MANEY'S
CONFEDERATE BRIGADE
AT THE
BATTLE OF
PERRYVILLE

STUART W. SANDERS

Charleston · London

THE
History
PRESS

Published by The History Press
Charleston, SC 29403
www.historypress.net

Copyright © 2014 by Stuart W. Sanders
All rights reserved

First published 2014

Manufactured in the United States

ISBN 978.1.62619.264.5

Library of Congress CIP data applied for.

CONTENTS

PREFACE

On October 8, 1862, more than 40,000 Union and Confederate soldiers clashed at Perryville, Kentucky. In the five-hour battle, more than 7,500 men were killed and wounded. Of the troops who fought at Perryville, perhaps none endured as much as the Tennessee and Georgia soldiers who composed Brigadier General George Maney's brigade. This Confederate unit entered the fray to save other Southern regiments; in doing so, it experienced the hardest fighting of the day. In battling two different Union brigades, Maney's men attacked—and captured—two enemy artillery positions, killed two Northern generals and nearly broke the Federal left flank. Many of Maney's regiments suffered 50 percent casualties, and several members of the unit, including Private Sam Watkins of the 1st Tennessee Infantry, called Perryville the hardest fight that they experienced during the entire Civil War.

The Battle of Perryville was Kentucky's most important battle, and Maney's Brigade played the most critical part. Tasked to break the Union left flank, these Confederates were nearly successful in rolling over that end of the Federal battle line. Had it not been for sheer exhaustion and staggering casualties, these Confederates could have won a clear victory at Perryville. Instead, their failure to break the enemy line helped keep the Bluegrass State in Union hands for the remainder of the war.

Maney's Brigade is the perfect lens through which to view the Battle of Perryville. Moreover, an examination of this unit provides a ground-level view of what the soldiers endured. In addition to showcasing the hardest fighting of the battle, this brigade's actions highlight the importance of regimental colonels, junior officers and aides. These men took the initiative and led the troops forward at crucial times. Had it not been for these officers, Maney's Brigade would have faltered early in the fight.

For nearly a decade, I was honored to work for the Perryville Battlefield Preservation Association (PBPA), a nonprofit organization charged with preserving and interpreting Kentucky's largest Civil War battleground. When The History Press published my first book, *Perryville Under Fire: The Aftermath of Kentucky's Largest Civil War Battle*, I acknowledged a number of people from the PBPA, the Perryville Battlefield Commission, state and local entities and the community of Perryville who were supportive during my tenure there. I still greatly appreciate their support and friendship.

Several friends and archivists helped with supplying illustrations and maps. Many thanks to Bob Glass, Centre College; Jennifer Duplaga, Kentucky Historical Society; Kurt Holman, Perryville Battlefield State Historic Site; Marsha Mullin, The Hermitage; and Myers Brown. Additional thanks go to Jim Campi and Griffith Waller at the Civil War Trust, who allowed me to republish the Civil War Trust's excellent maps. And a most sincere appreciation goes to Charley Pallos, who created a number of maps used in this book.

I am also grateful to Kirsten Schofield, Ryan Finn and the rest of the staff at The History Press who have helped make this project possible.

Importantly, this book could not have been completed without Kurt Holman, manager of the Perryville Battlefield State Historic Site. No one knows the Battle of Perryville as well as Kurt, and I am grateful for his expertise, his generosity with his research files and for his suggestions to this manuscript. His insight has been invaluable, and I appreciate his support and friendship.

I am grateful for supportive friends Erik Drake and Mignon Brousseau, Steve and Amy Isola and John and Andrea Mesplay. I am also appreciative of Jackson, Harrison, Mary Elizabeth and Lenox, all of whom said that they want to be mentioned in a book. Additional thanks go to Brian Grimmer, Gary Neighbors, Cindy Neighbors, Brian Neighbors, Heather Neighbors, Mark Read, Harv Smith, Robert H. Williams and W.L. Wilson. Much appreciation goes to my brother, Wallace Sanders, and my sister-in-law, Catherine Edwards Sanders.

I appreciate the encouragement of my friend Don Rightmyer and his wife, Bonnie, both of whom read the manuscript. I appreciate their help and friendship.

I am incredibly thankful to my wife, Jenny, and my children, John, Anne and Elizabeth, for their patience, love, encouragement and support.

Finally, I thank my parents. My father, Dr. I. Taylor Sanders II, taught history at Washington and Lee University for forty-two years, and my mother, Barbara Sanders, is a former English teacher. I am appreciative of their editorial skills but even more thankful to have them as parents. For their constant help and support, I dedicate this book to them.

Chapter 1

ON TO KENTUCKY

On October 9, 1862, one day after Kentucky's largest Civil War battle raged near Perryville, Confederate Major General Leonidas Polk walked through the arched doors of St. Philip's Episcopal Church in Harrodsburg. The Confederates had retreated ten miles to this city after the Battle of Perryville, and the town's courthouse, hotels, businesses and private homes were already crammed with hundreds of wounded Rebel soldiers. Polk had good reason to enter the church; in addition to commanding the Confederate right wing at Perryville, he was also an Episcopal bishop. Therefore, local legend holds, the bishop-general placed a guard around the church to ensure that it remained a house of worship rather than becoming full of maimed soldiers. After the horrific struggle at Perryville, the men needed a sanctuary to pray.[1]

Reverend Charles Quintard, the chaplain of the 1st Tennessee Infantry Regiment, part of Brigadier General George Earl Maney's brigade, accompanied the general. Quintard wrote, "I think that we both felt that we were in the presence of God. General Polk threw his arms about my neck and said: 'Oh, for the blessed days when we walked in the house of God as friends! Let us have prayer!'" Quintard had just endured hours in a field hospital helping his wounded comrades, and time in a church was a welcome respite.

Polk knelt at the altar railing as Quintard "vested myself with surplice and stole" and began praying. The chaplain then turned to Polk and "pronounced the benediction from the office for the visitation of the sick." As Quintard blessed the general, Polk remained kneeling at the altar and wept, his tears the culmination of fatigue, sadness and bitterness. During the Battle of Perryville, the bishop-general had sent one of his divisions into what was perhaps the most desperate charge to occur in Kentucky during the Civil War. In fact, many of the veterans who survived the fight recalled that Perryville was one of the most intense battles of the entire conflict.[2]

Quintard—and many of the troops who recalled the desperation of the fight—were members of Brigadier General George Earl Maney's brigade. With about 1,700 troops at Perryville, Maney's Brigade was part of Major General Benjamin Franklin Cheatham's division and was composed of the 1st, 6th, 9th and 27th Tennessee and the 41st Georgia Infantry Regiments. These men played a critical role at Perryville by shoving back the Union left flank in multiple, ferocious charges. Had it not been for a stubborn Federal defense late in the day, Maney's Brigade would have rolled up that side of the Union line and cut off the Federal right flank. Because this brigade experienced some of the heaviest fighting—with several regiments losing nearly 50 percent of their strength—they are the perfect lens through which to view the battle and, subsequently, to gain a greater understanding of the fight.

The prelude to General Polk's tears began after more than twenty-three thousand Union and Confederate soldiers were killed and wounded at the Battle of Shiloh, fought in southwestern Tennessee. Although the Confederate army, under the command of General Albert Sidney Johnston, bloodied Brigadier General Ulysses S. Grant's Federal army, Johnston's death and the timely arrival of Union reinforcements under the command of Major General Don Carlos Buell forced the exhausted Rebels back to Corinth, Mississippi.

Although Corinth was a defensible location, illness was prevalent. Private Sam Watkins of Maney's 1st Tennessee Infantry Regiment wrote that at Corinth, "We became starved skeletons; naked and ragged rebels. The chronic diarrhoea became the scourge of the army. Corinth became one vast hospital. Almost the whole army attended the sick call every morning. All the water courses went dry, and we used water out of filthy pools." With Federal troops inching toward the city, the Confederates fell back to Tupelo, fifty-two miles to the south. Watkins was pleased to reach Tupelo. He recalled, "We bade farewell to Corinth. Its history was black and dark and damning. No little speck of green oasis ever enlivened the dark recesses of our memory while at this place…It was but one vast graveyard that entombed the life and spirit of once brave and chivalrous men."[3]

Troops under the command of Brigadier General George Earl Maney played a critical role during the Battle of Perryville. Maney's Brigade, which successfully took two important Union positions, suffered some of the heaviest casualties during Kentucky's largest battle. Later, Maney fought a duel to defend himself against charges that he had shirked his duty at Perryville. *Courtesy of the Hermitage: Home of President Andrew Jackson, Nashville, Tennessee.*

While in Tupelo, Confederate General Braxton Bragg, who had recently been given command of the Rebel army, reorganized his newly named Army of the Mississippi. Major General Benjamin F. Cheatham's division was expanded to include four brigades, including Maney's Brigade. Cheatham's Division and Brigadier General Jones Withers's division formed the right wing of the army, commanded by the "bishop-general" Leonidas Polk. The other wing, commanded by Major General William Hardee, consisted of divisions commanded by Brigadier General James Patton Anderson and Major General Simon Bolivar Buckner. According to Hardee's assistant inspector general, "Some time was spent around Tupelo in the reorganization, instruction, and drill of this army by General Bragg, resulting in great betterment to its morale, drill and general efficiency." John W. Carroll of Maney's 27th Tennessee Infantry stated, "The ordeal of battle [Shiloh] and reorganization having been gone through with [*sic*] we began drilling daily. More regard was paid to discipline." The troops were beginning to feel like veterans.[4]

In the following months, this drill and discipline would be needed. In early June, the Federals who had pressured the Confederates at Corinth divided their massive army. Generals Grant, William T. Sherman and William S. Rosecrans threatened central Mississippi, but the Army of the Ohio, commanded by Major General Don Carlos Buell, pressed toward Chattanooga.[5]

Confederate officers recognized the importance of Chattanooga. The city was a crucial railroad hub that connected east Tennessee with Virginia and Georgia. Union possession of Chattanooga would cut the Confederate army off from military supplies stockpiled in Georgia and give the Federal army access to invade that state. If the city fell, Bragg could be cut off from half of the South's eight arsenals, located in Atlanta, Augusta, Macon and Columbus. In addition, Union control of east Tennessee, which would be ensured if Buell reached Chattanooga, would allow Unionist elements there to rally to the Stars and Stripes. Since the outbreak of the war, President Lincoln had sought a way to redeem the Unionist populace of east Tennessee. The president even stated, "If we can hold Chattanooga and Eastern Tennessee, I think that the rebellion must dwindle and die." The area produced wheat for the Confederacy, and the region's saltpeter, lead, coal and copper fueled the Southern war machine. If Chattanooga fell to the Army of the Ohio, industries in Georgia and South Carolina would lose these supplies. Bragg feared Buell's movements toward the region, stating that Buell's advance "threatened the very heart of our country, and was destined, unless checked immediately, to sever our main line of connection between the East and West."[6]

Shortly after assuming command of the army, Bragg received a panicked dispatch from Major General Edmund Kirby Smith, the commander of the Army of Kentucky, operating in east Tennessee. "Buell is reported crossing the river at Decatur and daily sending a regiment by rail toward Chattanooga," Smith wrote. "I have no force to repel such an attack." As Buell's army lumbered toward the city, Smith informed Bragg that the "successful holding of Chattanooga depends upon your co-operation."[7]

To plan a coordinated campaign to thwart Buell, Bragg and Smith met in Chattanooga on July 31. The two officers decided that Smith's army would capture the Union-controlled Cumberland Gap, while Bragg moved into middle Tennessee to strike toward Nashville. Once the Gap fell, Smith would rejoin Bragg's army, and their combined force would then crush Buell. If the Army of the Ohio was defeated at Nashville, the Confederates would then enter Kentucky and press toward Louisville or Cincinnati. Once in the Bluegrass State, the two Rebel armies would operate independently until they could meet in central Kentucky.[8]

Just as Lincoln had hoped to redeem east Tennessee, Confederate authorities were equally enthralled with the idea of seizing Kentucky. The Bluegrass State could provide horses and supplies for Rebel armies, and an

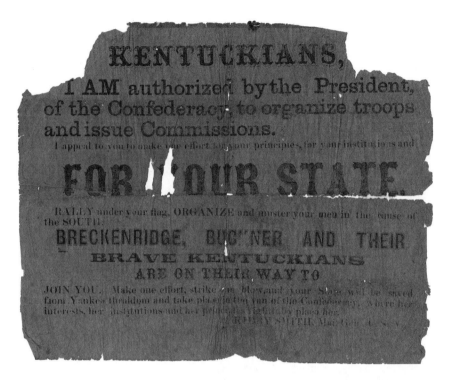

When multiple Confederate armies invaded Kentucky in the summer of 1862, they were convinced that thousands of recruits would join their ranks. This recruiting broadside from Confederate General Edmund Kirby Smith's army called for "Brave Kentuckians" to enlist. *Courtesy of the Kentucky Historical Society.*

occupied commonwealth would provide a buffer between the midwestern states and the Deep South. In addition, Confederate forces could advance into Indiana or Ohio, thereby influencing autumn congressional elections in favor of the Peace Democrats. Moreover, a recent raid into Kentucky by Confederate Colonel John Hunt Morgan led Confederate authorities to believe that if Kentucky were held, thousands of recruits would flock to the Southern banner. Morgan told Smith that if Rebel armies advanced, "25,000 or 30,000 men will join you at once." Finally, as Smith informed Confederate President Jefferson Davis, a Bluegrass invasion would "involve the abandonment of Middle Tennessee by the Federals" and would pull Buell away from Chattanooga.[9]

Although the plan called for Smith to help Bragg fight Buell near Nashville, Smith instead decided to invade the Bluegrass State. On August 13, after forcing Union troops away from Cumberland Gap,

HEADQ'RS TRANS-MISSISSIPPI DEPARTMENT, SHREVEPORT, LA., April 21, 1865.

Soldiers of the Trans-Mississippi Army:

The crisis of our revolution is at hand. Great disasters have overtaken us. The Army of Northern Virginia and our Commander-in-Chief are prisoners of war. With you rests the hope of our nation, and upon your action depends the fate of our people. I appeal to you in the name of the cause you have so heroically maintained—in the name of your firesides and families so dear to you—in the name of your bleeding country, whose future is in your hands. Show that you are worthy of your position in history. Prove to the world that your hearts have not failed in the hour of disaster, and that at the last moment you will sustain the holy cause which has been so gloriously battled for by your brethren east of the Mississippi.

You possess the means of long resisting invasion. You have hopes of succor from abroad. Protract the struggle, and you will surely receive the aid of nations who already deeply sympathize with you.

Stand by your colors—maintain your discipline. The great resources of this Department, its vast extent, the numbers, the discipline, and the efficiency of the army, will secure to our country terms that a proud people can with honor accept, and may, under the providence of God, be the means of checking the triumph of our enemy, and securing the final success of our cause.

E. KIRBY SMITH, General.

When Confederate General Edmund Kirby Smith led an army into Kentucky in the summer of 1862, he called it a "bold move, offering brilliant results." Smith's army, which was not present at the Battle of Perryville, won a major victory at the Battle of Richmond, Kentucky. *Courtesy of the Kentucky Historical Society.*

Smith moved into Kentucky. "My advance is made in the hope of permanently occupying Kentucky," he wrote. "It is a bold move, offering brilliant results." On August 30, his army crushed a Federal command at Richmond, Kentucky. Elated by the victory, Smith then took Lexington and Frankfort, the only pro-Union state capital to fall into Confederate hands during the war.[10]

Upon learning that Smith had marched northward into Kentucky, Bragg abandoned his plan of striking Buell at Nashville. The Tennessee capital was well fortified, and Bragg feared that Smith, operating alone in Kentucky, would be cut off and destroyed. Therefore, on August 28, Bragg moved into Kentucky. The march, however, was arduous. Lieutenant James I. Hall of Maney's 9th Tennessee Infantry noted that when the army neared Sparta, Tennessee, the slow Rebel wagon trains failed to catch up. Hunger struck the ranks, and Hall was offered a dollar for his only biscuit, which he declined. Luckily for the troops, division commander Frank Cheatham came to the rescue and purchased an entire field of corn. Hall related that some of the soldiers were so famished that they ate six to eight ears.[11]

Despite these hardships, many of the soldiers joked with one another to pass the time. One member of Maney's 9th Tennessee recalled that Hugh Hamner, a five-foot-four soldier, turned to Jim Rucker, who was six-foot-seven. "Rucker," Hamner asked, "what kind of weather have you got up there?" Rucker spat on Hamner's hat and replied, "It's raining up here, Hugh." The soldier remarked that this "created a loud laugh among all who heard it. It required but little of an alleged wit to cause a laugh among wearied soldiers."[12]

Jovial attitudes did little to improve the strain of the march. In addition to the lack of food, a drought affected Bragg's soldiers. One trooper remarked that "frequently, while we who were in the cavalry were watering our horses by companies, the infantry and artillerists would fill their canteens from under the horses with water which was wholly unfit for stock to drink. No doubt that much sickness and many deaths were attributable to the impure water." Lieutenant Hall of the 9th Tennessee agreed. He wrote that the troops drank water "so muddy that we could not see our faces in it."[13]

After advancing to Glasgow, Kentucky, in mid-September, Bragg's army besieged a Union garrison at Munfordville that capitulated. With Union positions falling in Kentucky with the Rebel advance, Buell feared that his supplies in Louisville were in danger. Believing that "Nashville

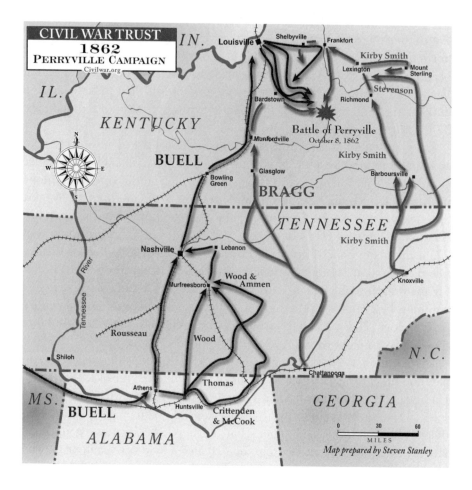

Union and Confederate troop movements during the 1862 Kentucky Campaign. *Courtesy of the Civil War Trust.*

can be held and Kentucky rescued," Buell's Army of the Ohio also advanced into the Bluegrass State. Bragg's delay around Munfordville gave Buell the time to rush to Louisville and protect that city. There, Buell integrated tens of thousands of recruits into his army, which he completely reorganized. With the opportunity to strike Louisville having slipped through his fingers, Bragg marched his men to Bardstown, forty miles southeast of Louisville.[14]

Chapter 2

ON TO PERRYVILLE

By early October 1862, multiple Confederate armies were operating in Kentucky, and three-fourths of the commonwealth was under Rebel control. Therefore, Buell moved to shove the Confederates from the state. Keeping his sights on Bragg's army at Bardstown, Buell, on October 1, sent most of his command—fifty-eight thousand men divided into three corps—toward Bardstown. To keep Bragg and Smith divided, Buell sent twenty thousand soldiers from Louisville toward Frankfort. It was an effective diversion.[15]

Bragg, who had gone to Frankfort to inaugurate a new Confederate governor of Kentucky, believed that the twenty thousand Union troops moving toward Frankfort was Buell's main army. Therefore, he ordered General Polk, his second in command, to move from Bardstown to strike those Federals near Versailles. Polk, however, worried about the Union troops at his front. With Confederate pickets reporting a large enemy force moving on Bardstown, Polk withdrew to the east. Concerned that Polk was not advancing against the Union troops near Frankfort, Bragg rushed to Harrodsburg, forty miles east of Bardstown, and ordered Polk to concentrate there.[16]

Federal troops reached Bardstown on October 4. Union Major General George Thomas reported that the town fell "after a pretty sharp skirmish of our advance cavalry." Although the Confederates had withdrawn, the Federals captured several Rebels who were too ill to travel, including W. Gardner, R.L. Smith and C. Dempsey of Maney's 9th Tennessee. Unlike

Union Major General Don Carlos Buell had three corps present for the Battle of Perryville, yet only one-third of his command was actively engaged. *Courtesy of the Library of Congress.*

Gardner or Dempsey, Smith never left Bardstown alive. He died in a hospital there on October 17. Within days, many more of Maney's command would become casualties.[17]

As the Confederates fell back to the east, they halted in Perryville, a small riverside village of three hundred inhabitants, located ten miles southwest of Harrodsburg. There were several reasons why the Rebels halted at Perryville. First, despite the drought, Perryville's Chaplin River and some local springs held water. Second, an extensive road network ran through the town and provided the Rebels with an easy escape route. Finally, the Southerners wanted to stay between the Union army and a supply depot that they had established at Camp Dick Robinson in Bryantsville, thirty miles to the east. In case they needed to abandon Kentucky for Tennessee, Confederate commanders knew that they would have to protect those supplies. According to Confederate Major General William Hardee, "The position at Perryville is strong, and offered many tactical and strategical [*sic*] advantages."[18]

When Cheatham reached town "late in the night," Hardee placed Cheatham's three brigades, including Maney's regiments, on the left of

This postwar image shows Merchants' Row, which was Perryville's main commercial district. In October 1862, Perryville had three hundred residents, many of whom fled town to avoid the impending battle. After the fight, most of these structures became makeshift hospitals. *Courtesy of Centre College.*

the Confederate line, on the south side of town. The troops camped with their lines partially extending through the village. Private Marcus Toney of Maney's 1st Tennessee Infantry said that his regiment "bivouacked after midnight in the suburbs of the little town of Perryville." Having previously camped in a cemetery at Munfordville, Toney wrote, "When we formed in line and stacked guns for a few hours' rest, Company B was again in a cemetery. Was it a bad omen that twice recently our company slept in a cemetery?"[19]

When the troops reached Perryville, the Confederates found the village to be deserted. Private Sam Watkins, also of the 1st Tennessee, realized that residents had fled town to avoid an impending fight. Watkins wrote, "I think all of the citizens of Perryville were taken with a sudden notion of promiscuous visiting about this time; at least they were not at home to all callers." That night, William Brown of Stanford's Mississippi Battery rode through downtown Perryville. "The houses were dark and as silent as a church yard," Brown recalled. "As I rode through the streets there was not even a dog to bark at me. It was a striking picture of a deserted village. All the townspeople had left to get clear of the expected battle." Several Confederates used this opportunity to procure supplies from abandoned homes and farms.[20]

Buell continued to press the Confederates and reached Perryville on October 7. His three corps converged on the town. Major General Thomas L. Crittenden's corps was approaching Perryville from the south, Major General Charles Gilbert's corps was west of town and Major General Alexander McCook's corps neared Perryville from the north. In the early morning hours of October 8, an advance unit of Arkansas soldiers fought a sharp skirmish west of town against Gilbert's advancing

Confederate General Braxton Bragg led his Army of the Mississippi into Kentucky in the summer of 1862. His campaign to hold Kentucky ended after the Battle of Perryville. *Courtesy of the Kentucky Historical Society.*

troops. The Confederates held a ridge overlooking Doctor's Creek, but the Federals shoved them back and claimed the hill and the creek's stagnant pools of water. With shots fired at Perryville, Confederate officers there, including Polk and Hardee, decided to assume a defensive position to see how events would develop.[21]

Still unaware that Buell's main army was converging on Perryville and irritated that Polk had assumed a defensive stance, Bragg rushed the ten miles from Harrodsburg to Perryville and realigned the Southern army. Bragg still believed that he faced an insignificant Union force at Perryville, so he determined to attack. He ordered Cheatham's Division to move north to form the Confederate right. These soldiers were to deploy next to Buckner's Division, which was north of the Mackville Road. As the Rebels did not expect much Federal activity south of town, Colonel Joseph Wheeler's cavalry guarded the Lebanon Road. To deal with the Union presence west of town, two brigades from Patton Anderson's division, led by Brigadier General Daniel W. Adams and Colonel Samuel Powell, were placed on the Springfield Road. J. Stoddard Johnston later wrote that Bragg, "still in ignorance of [Buell's] plans," ordered the attack to commence.[22]

Bragg decided to attack *en echelon*, with his divisions striking the eastward-facing Federal line from north to south, respectively. His troops would form a long, westward-facing line that ran from north to south. Cheatham's Division would begin the attack by striking the Union left, or the northern end of the enemy line. Then, two of Patton Anderson's brigades would strike the Union center while Buckner's Division rolled up the Union right. Finally, Powell's brigade would hit farther to the south, striking the Union troops who were massing west of town near Peter's Hill. The Southern assault would be made by little more than sixteen thousand men.[23]

Chapter 3

"THE ONSLAUGHT WAS TERRIBLE"

About midday," Brigadier General George Maney wrote, his 1,650 soldiers moved from the Confederate left to the far right with the rest of Cheatham's Division. The troops marched out of Perryville and trod northward up the Harrodsburg Pike. Moving down a slope to the dry Chaplin River, the soldiers passed the Crawford Spring, one of the few viable water sources in the area, near where Bragg had established his headquarters. The troops then marched down a farm road lined with limestone fences that hugged the riverbank, moving north to take their place on the Southern right flank.[24]

Union troops were still arriving on the north side of Perryville. As Major General Alexander McCook's corps filed into position on the hills there, Union division commander Brigadier General Lovell Rousseau and artilleryman Captain Cyrus Loomis formed their troops on a ridge above Doctor's Creek, a dry, tree-lined stream that wound past the farmhouse of Henry P. Bottom. As Cheatham's Division marched northward, Rousseau and Loomis spotted immense clouds of dust rising from the Confederate troop movements. Believing that the clouds were stirred up by Bragg's army retreating to Harrodsburg, Loomis said, "I guess we have tread on the tail of Mr. Bragg's coat, ha, ha!" Since the Rebels had withdrawn from Bardstown to Springfield and then to Perryville, many Union troops who saw the dust clouds believed that the Southerners were continuing their retreat. They could not have been more mistaken.[25]

Cheatham's Division followed the wall-lined road that coiled alongside the Chaplin River. Moving across a farm owned by the fifty-five-year-old Jacob Goodnight, the division reached another farm owned by the Walker family. Cheatham likely established his headquarters in the Walker home, a brick structure located on a hill above the river. The Confederates then formed battle lines in the fields near a twist in the Chaplin River called Walker's Bend, located west of the house. As the soldiers trailed onto the farm, one member of Brigadier General Daniel Donelson's brigade noted, "[A]bout this time the artillery opened up." It was nearly noon.[26]

In order to soften the Union lines before the infantry attack, the Southerners bombarded the Federal position with cannon fire. At noon, Confederate Captain William Carnes's Tennessee artillery battery deployed on a ridge south of Walker's Bend and fired on McCook's center with four six-pounder cannons. Union Captain Peter Simonson, commander of the 5th Battery, Indiana Light Artillery, was discussing recent campaigns with a newspaper reporter when the bombardment commenced. The reporter wrote that the two men were chatting when "a spherical shot buried itself deep in the side of the hill, just below where we were standing, and a half dozen more whistled fiercely over our heads and raised great clouds of dust as they struck in the dried up fields beyond." The Union gunners quickly jumped into action. Two Federal artillery batteries—Simonson's battery and Loomis's 1st Battery, Michigan Light Artillery—responded from a ridge about one mile away from the Rebel guns. For more than an hour, the batteries dueled, but the Union artillerymen, firing rifled pieces against the Confederates' smoothbores, held the advantage. The Federal shells accurately exploded among the Southern cannon, and several Confederate artillerymen were killed. Eventually, Captain Thomas Stanford's Mississippi battery also joined the barrage, but it did little to stem the Union advantage.

One of Stanford's artillerymen, William A. Brown, recalled that "[t]he battery we were fighting was in position something over a mile distant. The smoke from their guns was all we could see. They had the advantage in the fight, as they already had our range, and every shot was well aimed…an unlucky shell stretched out three of our boys on the ground." Because only a handful of Confederate cannons had fired on the Union position, the Northerners mistakenly believed that the artillery covered a Confederate retreat. Again, the secessionists had accidentally reinforced the Federal assumption that they were leaving Perryville. Although the Southern artillery caused little damage, the duel was successful in forcing the Federal batteries to expend a large amount of their long-range ammunition.[27]

For Lieutenant George Landrum of the 2nd Ohio Infantry, the duel was an exciting exchange. The officer called it "a fine artillery duel." When the shells fell too close, he nervously "could not help laughing. There was an excitement now to me about it; at first a sort of cold chill ran down my back, my hair seemed to be raising my hat off my head." When the cannon fire stopped, the Buckeye "supposed they had brought the battery there to cover their retreat, as I had lost all faith in their fighting us."[28]

When the duel ended, a correspondent from the *Cincinnati Gazette* remarked, "In fact there was a lull in the battle about this time all over the field, but it was the lull which follows the first blast of a tempest and indicates that it is gathering its forces for a more terrible onset."[29]

While Cheatham's regiments prepared for battle, Captain Thomas H. Malone, Maney's adjutant, used this opportunity to catch up on some much-needed sleep. Malone, kept busy attending to his duties, had not slept the night before. Curled up on the ground, Malone wrote, "I was rudely awakened by Emmett Cockrill with the expression: 'Get up, you damned fool! You'll get your brains knocked out!' and I found that I was lying right in the rear of the lane and a shell which I had not heard had exploded and covered my face with dirt…A distant battery was throwing heavy shells to points where we might be supposed to be located." To sleep in the midst of such fire details the Confederate's severe exhaustion.[30]

One member of Brigadier General Daniel Donelson's 38th Tennessee also recalled the danger during the deployment, but these veterans, like Malone, were relaxed in spite of the fire. He wrote that "[s]ome of the boys began to crack walnuts while the shells and long-range Minies were dropping around and whistling overhead." The division commander was also calm. Brown of Stanford's Battery noted, "Not far from us Gen. Cheatham sat on his horse in the midst of his staff, calmly smoking his pipe."[31]

Although many of the shells passed safely overhead, the artillery fire from the duel was dangerous. Lieutenant Colonel William Frierson, commander of Maney's 27th Tennessee Infantry, remarked that as his regiment marched to the Walker farm "under a very hot sun," the artillery rained fire on them. He wrote that "for a mile before the engagement commenced the men were continually exposed to the fire of the enemy's batteries." When the brigade formed near a building that had been earmarked for use as a hospital (likely the Walker home), one private was killed and several more were injured in Lieutenant Colonel John Buford's 9th Tennessee Infantry.[32]

Many of Cheatham's veterans, despite the casualties, displayed coolness under this fire. According to Hardee's assistant inspector general, the soldiers' past combat experience and the constant marching of the campaign had whipped them into excellent shape. He wrote that "the Confederate army was never in better trim for battle." Within hours, their endurance would be severely tested.[33]

During the lull that occurred after the artillery duel, most of the Federals believed that the Rebels were retreating to Harrodsburg. George Landrum of the 2nd Ohio wrote, "We all supposed they were leaving, as we could see nothing of them." The Northerners, however, were mistaken. Several hundred yards to the east, Bragg's Southerners prepared their attack.[34]

Brigadier General Daniel Donelson's Tennessee brigade, which was part of Cheatham's Division, would lead the Southern assault. Although Donelson had five infantry regiments under his command, only three were present when the attack commenced. Bragg had detached Donelson's 8th and 51st Tennessee Infantry Regiments and Captain William Carnes's battery prior to the artillery duel. While Carnes bombarded the Union lines, the 8th and 51st Tennessee supported the cannons. Therefore, only Donelson's 15th, 16th and 38th Tennessee Infantry Regiments were present for the assault, meaning that the opening Rebel attack was made by an understrength brigade. The three regiments were, however, veteran units. The 15th and 38th had fought at Shiloh, and the 16th Tennessee had served at Cheat Mountain. Immediately prior to the attack, Donelson had sent his assistant adjutant general to retrieve Carnes's Battery and the detached regiments, but these units did not rejoin the brigade when Donelson deployed.[35]

Bragg planned for his brigades to successively pound the Union line from north to south. Bragg first wanted to strike the Union left flank, or the northern end of the enemy line, but before his infantry could attack, he had to determine where the Union left flank ended. Therefore, Confederate Colonel John Wharton's cavalry, consisting of the 8th Texas Cavalry and elements of the 4th Tennessee Cavalry and 1st Kentucky Cavalry, swept across the hills west of the Chaplin River to reconnoiter the Federal position. As Wharton's horsemen galloped through the pastures, Union Captain David Stone's Battery A, Kentucky Light Artillery, and Captain Asahel Bush's 4th Battery, Indiana Light Artillery, which had been posted next to the Benton Road near the Dixville Crossroads, lobbed shells at Wharton's troopers. Upon returning to the Rebel lines, the cavalrymen reported that these guns anchored the Northerners' left. Unfortunately for the Confederates, when Wharton made his report, Union Brigadier General James S. Jackson's division reached the battlefield from Mackville. As these soldiers—members of Brigadier General William Terrill's brigade—arrived, they were placed on a high ridge several hundred yards west of Stone's battery, a deployment that extended the Union left flank. Therefore, when the Confederates attacked, Donelson's opening assault moved more toward the Union center, rather than striking the extreme left of the Federal line. It was an error that nearly destroyed the Confederate plan.[36]

Wharton's cavalry rode out to drive off Federal pickets and prepare the way for Donelson's attack. As the horsemen galloped from north to south, they encountered skirmishers from Union Colonel Leonard Harris's 33rd Ohio Infantry. Men from the 10th Ohio and 2nd Ohio were also sent forward toward the Chaplin River as skirmishers, and Harris later reported that they were "well advanced to the front in the woods."[37]

At least two Buckeyes were particularly surprised by the Rebel horsemen. Thinking that the Confederates were gone, E.W. Gilbert of Company K, 33rd Ohio, and a comrade took their company's canteens and walked northward, looking for water. They found "a pool of water which the hogs had been wallowing in. We drove the hogs out, and proceeded to fill the canteens. The water was thick with mud, but that was the best we could find." After filling half of the canteens, Confederate cavalry crested a nearby hill and galloped toward them, shooting. Gilbert was nearly captured until Federal cannons fired, their shells shredding "the limbs of the trees." The horsemen fled. "This battery saved our hides from bullet holes," Gilbert added.[38]

Sputtering musketry and the crackling of pistol shots continued as Wharton's cavalry encountered the 33rd Ohio's skirmishers. John M. Claiborne, a member of Terry's Texas Rangers, commented that "every man [was] doing his level best to get in first and do all the damage he possibly could by staying in and shooting all the time and hitting a man in a vital spot every time he shot." The Buckeyes gave as well as they received. According to Ohioan Angus Waddle, the skirmishers fired and "emptied many of their saddles and caused them to quickly disappear." Although these cavalrymen paved the way for Donelson's attack, the Confederates were still unaware that McCook's left flank had been extended.[39]

Donelson's Tennesseans climbed the bluffs above the Chaplin River and gathered on the flat land immediately west of the banks. There,

Maney's Brigade was part of Confederate Major General Leonidas Polk's wing of the Confederate Army of the Mississippi. In addition to being a Southern general, Polk was also an Episcopal bishop. *Courtesy of the Library of Congress.*

Donelson formed his three regiments into two lines. The 15th Tennessee was on the left of the first line, with the 16th Tennessee to its right and the 38th Tennessee behind it. Cheatham placed Brigadier General A.P. Stewart's command 400 yards behind Donelson's Brigade, and Maney's five regiments were 150 yards behind Stewart. As Donelson's men prepared to attack, the brigade commander reported that the troops were subjected to "a constant firing of the Enemy's Battery in position about a mile distant." Within minutes, this artillery tore his brigade apart.[40]

Because of the lack of additional cavalry reconnaissance, the rolling terrain and some woods that grew between the Union and Confederate lines, Cheatham could not see the Federal lines. Therefore, he ordered Donelson's Brigade to move toward the Federals' 5th Battery, Indiana Light Artillery, commanded by Captain Peter Simonson. Although Cheatham thought that this position anchored the Union left, this battery was more than four hundred yards away from the Yankees' left flank. Because of this error, Donelson careened more toward the center of the Northern line.[41]

As Donelson's Tennesseans deployed, the bishop-general Leonidas Polk grew euphoric. When Polk heard Cheatham exhort his troops to

"Give 'em hell, boys," the clergyman nearly forgot his holy station. "Give it to 'em boys," Polk shouted. "Give 'em what General Cheatham says!"[42]

Donelson's three regiments surged forward with a shout. J. Stoddard Johnston of Bragg's staff was near Cheatham's Division when the attack commenced. "The batteries and lines of battle of both sides could be seen distinctly," he wrote, "except when occasionally obscured by the dense smoke. Never was a battle scene more perfectly spread out to the eye, while the occasional whistling of a minie [ball] and the constant passage of shells near us, sometimes cutting the cedar twigs above our heads and sometimes bursting close by, served to remind us that we were not exempt from danger."[43]

When Donelson's lines crested the hill, the attack surprised the Federals, many of whom were cooking, relaxing or looking for water. Waddle commented that "a large force of gray-coated infantry were seen coming directly upon our flank. And now the battle was upon us." He added, "With closed columns and the rebel yell, which we then heard for the first time, they came like veterans and the onslaught was terrible." George Landrum of the 2nd Ohio gazed eastward with a telescope. He wrote, "Suddenly there emerged from the wood the head of a column of men, and as they came out, their bayonets glistened in the sun, and then I knew they were coming for us." It was about 2:00 p.m., and Donelson's men encountered the 33rd Ohio's skirmishers in a "skirt of woods" and drove them off. The Federal skirmishers pulled back to some trees, and the remainder of the regiment rushed to their support. Eventually, the Buckeyes regrouped near a fence closer to the rest of Union Colonel Leonard Harris's brigade.[44]

When Donelson pressed toward Samuel Harris's battery, the Federal soldiers on the extreme Union left were dumbfounded. Brigadier General William R. Terrill, leader of the 33rd Brigade, and his division commander, Brigadier General James S. Jackson, stood on a ridge with three infantry regiments and Lieutenant Charles Parsons' eight-gun artillery battery. As Samuel Harris's battery and Simonson's guns lobbed shells into Donelson's front, Terrill and Jackson ordered Parsons' cannons wheeled to the right. With Donelson's right flank less than three hundred yards away, the gunners aimed at the 16th Tennessee and fired. The Tennesseans moved down into a deep depression and pressed westward toward a cabin and barn owned by tenant farmer Mary Jane Gibson. Peppered on the front and right by artillery, the Rebels were shocked to discover that they were not striking the Union left. Polk recalled that the troops were "met by a storm of shot, shell, and musketry from several batteries strongly posted and supported by heavy masses of infantry." For Donelson's command, there was to be no envelopment of the Federal line. Instead, the men marched toward the Union center and certain annihilation.[45]

Fortunately for Donelson, Parsons' gunners were inexperienced artillerymen, having recently been pulled from the 105th Ohio Infantry Regiment. Therefore, Parsons' cannons probably did not damage Donelson's infantry; nonetheless, the psychological effect of being a lone, three-regiment brigade bombarded by several batteries must have crippled their morale. The leadership of regimental officers, however, propelled the men forward. It is likely that two colonels in particular—the experienced and hard-fighting Robert C. Tyler of the 15th Tennessee and John Savage of the 16th Tennessee—played critical roles in maintaining order. Confusion, however, soon erupted.[46]

Donelson was initially pleased with the advance. He wrote that "in making through the open field for more than ½ mile the Brigade was subjected to the cross firing of two of the Enemy's Batteries killing and wounding several. Although shot and shell fell in profusion there was no faltering on the part of men or officers." Colonel Savage remarked that as the brigade moved away from the bluffs overlooking the Chaplin River,

> I was riding in front expecting a surprise, the left of the regiment was at the edge of the forest and the field, when the battery, about one hundred and fifty yards from the regiment, fired, enfilading it, sweeping the whole length of the line, killing a captain, a lieutenant and many privates. I was riding in front of the regiment; a grape shot passed through the head of my horse below the eyes. Remembering to have seen thirty or forty riderless horses running over the field of Molino del Rey [during the Mexican-American War], I threw the bridle of my horse over a snag, took a Remington pistol from the holsters, and ordered the regiment forward to get out of range of the battery.[47]

To avoid the artillery, Donelson redirected his men to the right. This brisk change in direction, however, caused confusion. When the regiments shifted northward, the 16th Tennessee, on the right of Donelson's first line, accidentally moved ahead of the other two regiments. Therefore, despite the bombardment, the general halted his troops and reformed his lines. Poor communication under fire, however, contributed to errors. A member of Cheatham's staff reached the 16th Tennessee while Donelson was with another regiment. The staff officer hastily ordered the 16th to attack and moved the unit ahead of the rest of the brigade. Donelson later wrote, "The consequence was when this Regt. came within range of the Enemy's small arms, they received the first shock of the Enemy's fire." Lieutenant Jesse Walling of the 16th Tennessee expressed surprise "that every man in [our] regiment was not killed, as we fought the enemy to the front, left and right flanks unsupported."[48]

When the 16th Tennessee became separated from the other regiments, the slaughter was terrible. C.H. Clark noted that they were "falling dead and wounded all about me…school mates and playmates, neighbors and friends, and I thought all would be killed…I had no hope of getting out alive." Clark's comrade, Thomas Head, concurred. Head wrote that "the enemy opened a murderous fire upon [the 16th Tennessee] with musketry and artillery from right, left, and front. The ranks of the Sixteenth Regiment were mowed down at a fearful rate."[49]

The casualties angered the colonel of the 16th Tennessee. Savage, a native of Warren County, Tennessee, turned forty-seven years old the day after the battle. He was a veteran of the Seminole War and the Mexican-American War, where he had been wounded at Molino del Rey. A prewar lawyer and Tennessee's attorney general, Savage was also in the U.S. Congress in the 1840s and 1850s. Davis Biggs of the 16th Tennessee called him "a fine officer, a grizzled veteran of the Mexican War." Savage had organized the regiment, and its destruction at Perryville left him embittered toward Donelson, Cheatham and the Rebel high command. Savage blamed all of them for the losses.[50]

The Union fire affected one family especially. Company A of the 16th Tennessee was composed of men from McMinnville, Tennessee. This 148-man company contained 22 members of the Cantrell family, all of whom were brothers and cousins. Their captain was L.N. Savage, the younger brother of the regiment's colonel. When the battle ended, 4 of the Cantrells were dead and 2 more wounded. Families across the Volunteer State mourned losses from Perryville. Fighting alone and unsupported, the regiment suffered horrendous casualties. Of Savage's 370 men, 47 were killed and 179 wounded, a staggering loss of nearly 60 percent. This proved to be the highest percentage loss of any Confederate regiment that fought at Perryville.[51]

The severity of the crossfire also led to "a most remarkable wound." Corporal H.I. Hughes, Company F, 16th Tennessee, gave the Rebel yell as he charged. Screaming at the top of his lungs, Hughes was shot in the mouth, and all of his lower teeth were knocked out. "When taken from the field," a comrade wrote, "it was found that he had been hit in the mouth by two bullets at a cross-fire. They had met in his mouth and each ranged with the teeth of the lower jaw, lodging one on each side of his neck. His face was not marked on the outside." Another one of Donelson's wounded crawled behind a tree for shelter, but this proved to be insufficient cover. The unlucky soldier was killed by a Union canister round.[52]

Donelson's men moved into a long, flat valley between several ridges. Here, the 33rd Ohio, posted behind a fence about fifty yards away, fired into Donelson's left flank. Lieutenant Jesse Walling of the 16th Tennessee recalled that "[a]ll at once the enemy raised up from behind a rail fence, pouring a deadly fire into us and killing great numbers of our men." According to Savage, the Buckeye gunfire also killed Donelson's horse. "I ordered a charge," Savage wrote. "We drove the enemy from behind the fences, killing many of them as they fled." Dead and wounded Ohioans lay scattered among the rails, including Lieutenant Colonel Oscar Moore of the 33rd Ohio, who had been wounded in the leg. Moore, who refused "assistance to leave the field," was captured. The injury led to a unique reunion. Savage and Moore had served in the U.S. Congress together, and Savage ordered his personal surgeon to attend to the wounded Federal officer.[53]

Donelson pressed toward the Gibson cabin. Davis Biggs of the 38th Tennessee recalled moving "through a field where the grapeshot and shrapnel were rattling against the cornstalks, which had been cut and shocked up, also thinning our ranks." The horse of Colonel John Carter of the 38th Tennessee was killed. Carter was then injured in the leg and advanced on foot until he caught a riderless mount. Although Carter survived Perryville, his luck did not hold. He was later killed at the Battle of Franklin, Tennessee.[54]

Donelson's Brigade momentarily veered northward before readjusting to its original direction, moving westward toward the cabin. There, Savage was shot through the leg. Moments later, a canister round ricocheted off the building and knocked the officer senseless for an hour. Despite numerous Southern casualties, Donelson reported that the Unionists "were driven back with great slaughter for more than a mile…we had committed sad havoc in killing and wounding large numbers." Near the cabin, however, Donelson's attack ground to a halt. There, the Confederates were hit on the right by Samuel Harris's artillery and on their left by Leonard Harris's musketry. Thomas Head of the 16th Tennessee wrote, "The enemy bending his line around the right flank of the Sixteenth Tennessee Regiment near an old log cabin, an enfilading fire of musketry and artillery was poured into its ranks." Confederate James Thompson simply noted, "The battle now raged with terror and the slaughter was terrible." The price that Donelson paid for attacking with an understrength brigade was well illustrated by one company in the 16th Tennessee. These men went into the fight with eighty-four men. The next morning, only sixteen of these Tennesseans were "able for service."[55]

After the battle, Cincinnati war correspondent Alf Burnett traveled past the Gibson cabin. The scene described the severity of the fight. "About a mile and a half to the rear of the field of battle there stands, in a large, open field, a solitary log-house containing two rooms," Burnett wrote. "The house is surrounded by a fence inclosing a small patch of ground. The chimney had been partly torn away by a cannonball. The shell had struck the roof of the building, ripping open quite a gutter in the rafters. A dead horse lay in the little yard directly in front of the house, actually blocking the doorway, while shot and shell were scattered in every direction about the field in front and rear of this solitary homestead." Burnett encountered the cabin's residents, scurrying away from the battlefield with their belongings. The widow informed him that when the fighting started and bullets pattered off of the log house, she was so terrified that she took an axe, chopped a hole in the floor and hid between the joists with her children until the fighting ended.[56]

Bragg's attack was faltering. The arrival of additional Union troops had extended the Federal left flank. Therefore, Donelson's regiments were getting torn apart as they attacked toward the center of the enemy lines. In order for Bragg's plan to be successful, the Confederates would have to take the northern end of the Union line. It was an important job that would be tasked to Maney's Brigade.

Chapter 4

INTO BATTLE

I wondered why the fighting did not begin," Private Sam Watkins of the 1ˢᵗ Tennessee Infantry recalled. "Never on earth were our troops more eager for the engagement to open." Maney's Brigade was ready for a fight. Poised to enter the Battle of Perryville, the troops waited impatiently as Donelson's command opened the Confederate attack. Shortly, Maney's soldiers would also be embroiled in Kentucky's largest battle.[57]

Watkins and his fellow Rebels were led by an able commander. Maney, the son of Thomas and Rebecca Southall Maney, was born on August 24, 1826, in Franklin, Tennessee. After an early education at local schools, Maney attended the Nashville Seminary before graduating from the University of Nashville in 1845. George fought in the Mexican-American War as a lieutenant in the Nashville Blues, a Volunteer State infantry regiment, and left the service in 1848. Two years later, he was admitted to the Tennessee bar and opened a practice in Nashville. In 1853, he married Bettie Crutcher. Their union was blessed with two sons and three daughters.[58]

When the Civil War erupted, Maney volunteered for the Confederate army and was commissioned a captain in the 11ᵗʰ Tennessee Infantry. In May 1861, however, he was transferred to the 1ˢᵗ Tennessee and elected colonel. Known as the "Kid Glove Regiment," the 1ˢᵗ Tennessee established a formidable reputation early in the conflict. George D. Prentice, the fiery Unionist editor of the *Louisville Journal*, wrote that it was "such a pity [that] the magnificence [of the 1st Tennessee] was not displayed in a better cause."[59]

It quickly became evident that the regiment could endure great hardships. Organized in Nashville on May 9, 1861, the unit was mustered into Southern service on August 1. Of the twelve companies, each was known by a colorful *nom de guerre*. Companies A, B and C, from Nashville, were the Rock City Guards; members of Williamson County's Company D were the Williamson Grays; members of Company E, composed of Davidson County men, were the Tennessee Riflemen; members of F, from Nashville, were the Railroad Boys; members of G, from Maury and Hardin Counties, were the Brown Guards; members of Company H were the Maury Grays from Maury County; members of Company I were the Rutherford County Rifles; members of K, of Giles County, were the Martin Guards; members of Company L, which joined in May 1862, called themselves the Nashville Battalion.[60]

On July 13, 1861, Maney's 1st Tennessee departed the Volunteer State for the Old Dominion. Upon reaching Hillsboro, the troops rode the rails into northwestern Virginia, where they camped at Big Springs. The men formed a brigade with the 7th and 14th Tennessee Infantry Regiments, commanded by Brigadier General Samuel Anderson. After fighting at Cheat Mountain, the troops were deployed to Winchester. From January 1 until February 7, 1862, they marched with Brigadier General Thomas J. Jackson, the former Virginia Military Institute professor who had earned the nickname "Stonewall" at the Battle of First Manassas. Moving into Maryland to seek and destroy the enemy, the regiment endured a bitter winter. With no blankets, six inches of snow and the Potomac River frozen, one member of the regiment commented, "No command ever endured greater hardships than ours during this thirty-seven days." On February 19, however, the regiment left Jackson's command and returned to Tennessee. The men had gained military experience and built a formidable reputation at Cheat Mountain, Bath, Sewell Mountain, Brady's Gate, Romney and Hancock, Maryland. As it left western Virginia, the regiment was briefly split apart. Companies A through E were sent to Cumberland Gap, while the remaining troops traveled with Maney to Corinth and eventually fought at Shiloh. After this battle, the Tennesseans were reunited, and their command structure was reorganized with the rest of Bragg's army.[61]

Shiloh proved to be a great test for George Maney. Prior to the battle, he was handed Colonel William H. Stephens's 2nd Brigade when Stephens became too ill to fight. Maney, commanding the 1st, 6th, and 9th Tennessee Regiments and the 7th Kentucky Infantry, displayed leadership qualities that earned him permanent brigade command. Ordered to assault the strongly defended area known as the "Hornet's Nest," Maney directed his men to lie down in some woods near the Federal line. When the Federals opened fire and emptied their guns, Maney ordered his troops to charge. "The enemy could not wait to sustain the shock," Maney reported, "but broke in disorder and fled precipitately before us." Cheatham, Maney's future division commander, referred to this attack as "most brilliant, as it was certainly one of the most decisively successful" assaults of the battle. As Maney's regiments attacked across some fields owned by resident Sarah Bell, they charged against Captain William R. Terrill's Battery H, 5th United States Artillery. Maney's command was beaten back. Six months later, at the Battle of Perryville, Maney's men repaid Terrill for leaving, as one witness recalled, "piles of mangled bodies" in front of the Union cannons. For his service at Shiloh, Maney was awarded a brigadier general's star. On April 29, Colonel Hume R. Feild replaced Maney as regimental commander of the 1st Tennessee, John Patterson was named lieutenant colonel and John House became major of the regiment.[62]

By the time Bragg's army reorganized at Tupelo, Maney's Brigade consisted of the 1st, 6th and 9th Tennessee. The 7th Kentucky had left his command, but the Tennessee brigadier was given the 27th Tennessee and the 41st Georgia Infantry Regiments. Each of these units had a unique history. The 6th Tennessee was organized at Camp Beauregard in Jackson, Tennessee, in May 1861 and was recruited from Haywood, Madison and Fayette Counties. At Shiloh, where the troops fought at the infamous Hornet's Nest, the regiment suffered heavily, losing nearly 500 casualties. The previous summer, the command had consisted of 851 men, and at Perryville, little more than 300 soldiers composed this regiment.

The 9th Tennessee was also organized in Jackson that May, and these troops hailed from Haywood, Fayette, Tipton, Shelby, Hardeman, Weakley, Obion and Lauderdale Counties. When Company H of the 9th Tennessee was formed and was christened the "Obion Avalanche," 126 men joined the company. Of these, only 7 were slaveholders. Shiloh also bloodied this regiment, which lost 60 men. The next losses were incurred after Shiloh, when the soldiers' homes fell behind Federal lines, and many of the men deserted to join their families.[63]

Of Maney's new regiments, the 27th Tennessee was formed at Camp Trenton, Tennessee, in September 1861. These men were recruited from Benton, McNairy, Obion, Henderson, Decatur, Crockett, Weakley and Carroll Counties. At Shiloh, where they fought in S.A.M. Wood's brigade, they lost 54 percent of the 350 men who entered the battle. The 41st Georgia, with men from Cobb, Troup, Taylor and Heard Counties, was a green regiment that had been organized in the fall of 1861. At Perryville, it received a harsh baptism of fire.[64]

When Bragg's army was reorganized, an artillery battery was assigned to each brigade. Lieutenant William B. Turner's Mississippi battery, consisting of two six-pounder and two twelve-pounder artillery pieces, was assigned to Maney's Brigade. Turner's Battery would play a crucial role at Perryville.[65]

Maney's unit was assigned to Cheatham's Division, which consisted of four brigades. The tough-as-nails Cheatham had competent brigade commanders, including Brigadier Generals Daniel Donelson, Alexander P. Stewart and Maney and Colonel Preston Smith. Nearly all of Cheatham's infantrymen were Tennesseans, with the exception of Maney's Georgians and some Texans who served with Smith. Each brigade consisted of five infantry regiments.[66]

Maney, who had been friends with Cheatham since their prewar days in Nashville, knew of Cheatham's questionable reputation. Cheatham, a rugged fighter with a love of potent drink, profane language and a good scrap, had, according to historian Thomas L. Connelly, "a crudeness which did not appeal to Bragg." Bragg considered Cheatham to be a "stout, rather rough-looking man" and thought him to be unqualified for division command. After the Battle of Perryville, the two officers quickly became enemies in the rough-and-tumble political realm that was the Rebel army of the West.[67]

The constant marching of the Kentucky campaign had whipped Maney's Brigade into shape. Some of the men, however, were winded from their rushed trek from Perryville to Walker's Bend, the flat bottomland located at a curl in the Chaplin River north of town. "Tired and heated," Colonel William Frierson of the 27th Tennessee Infantry wrote, "the men were ordered to load and prepare for battle."[68]

Maney's Brigade was the second Confederate unit to enter the fray. With Donelson's troops caught in the withering crossfire near the center of the Union line, Maney's men were sent forward to correct the error and strike the Federal left. When the brigade moved toward the sound of battle, it encountered steep cliffs on the west side of the Chaplin River and became scattered. "The opposite bank of this creek directly in front of our approach was a precipitous bluff from twenty to forty feet high," Maney reported. "To ascend the bluff directly in front in anything like order would have been impossible." To avoid the bluffs, Confederate staff officers sent Maney's Brigade, accompanied by Lieutenant William Turner's four-gun battery, several hundred yards to the north to cross the river where the terrain was more accommodating. Once across the river, Maney wrote, the brigade was to "take possession of the woods on the highland beyond."[69]

To clear out any enemy soldiers, Confederate Colonel John Wharton's cavalry swept the woods where Maney's men were to deploy. Cheatham, Maney recalled, then ordered the brigade "[t]o advance as rapidly as practicable through the woods toward the enemy. Attack, drive and press him." Maney needed to silence Union Lieutenant Charles Parsons' eight cannons, destroy Brigadier General William Terrill's infantry brigade and envelop the Union left flank.[70]

The Rebels crossed the Chaplin River and bypassed the bluffs. According to Colonel George C. Porter of the 6th Tennessee Infantry, the brigade moved through a "thick wood," covered with brush and undergrowth. With the sound of gunfire gaining in intensity, the brigade formed in woods several hundred yards northeast of Parsons' artillery battery. It was hoped that Maney's command could succeed in what Donelson had failed to do: crush the Federal left flank.[71]

After crossing the river, Maney encountered several of Wharton's cavalrymen. Maney was unable to find Wharton among the riders, so the general ordered the horsemen to the far right to prevent them from hindering his infantry's movements. In addition, the general wanted the troopers to protect his right flank, located on the extreme northern end of his advancing line. A few minutes later, Maney found Wharton and explained that he had ordered several Rebel riders to the right. Wharton then sent his eight hundred cavalrymen to protect Maney's flank.[72]

When Maney halted to speak with Wharton, he lost track of his staff officers. Some had been sent to the rear with orders, while others were scattered throughout the brigade, keeping the ranks packed together as the men moved westward through the woods. Upon reaching a slight depression in the ground that was protected on its western side by a small swale, Maney formed his brigade into two battle lines. The cannons roared a few hundred yards away; Maney wrote, "I was informed [that] Genl. Donelson had become hotly engaged and was in great need of reinforcements. The action seemed but a short distance to my front and appeared to be fiercely waged with both Infantry and Artillery." Maney moved forward to examine the ground over which his brigade would attack.[73]

Maney easily found the enemy. He wrote that "[f]acing my approach and slightly to the right of Genl. Donelson's command was a strong battery placed on a hill top in a open field and less than one hundred and twenty yards from the nearest edge of the woods in which I was." From this position, "The battery was actively engaged [in firing] on Genl. Donelson's command at short range and partly in firing into the woods through which I was approaching."[74]

Before the advance continued, two soldiers in the 27th Tennessee— William Rhodes and Frank Buck, who was described as a "mere boy"—approached their captain, John Carroll. They told Carroll that they knew they would "be killed that day." Carroll wrote, "Their pale features, their calm demeanor, their determined looks impressed me much...I did offer that they take pass and drop out, which they refused to do." The two soldiers would not abandon their duty, and both moved forward with their command. Unfortunately, they proved to be accurate prophets.[75]

From the depression where Maney's command waited, the woods extended about four hundred yards to the west. The ground slightly undulated downward until the woods ended. There, at a split-rail fence that divided the woods from cleared pastureland, the terrain rose sharply to form a long ridge where Parsons' eight guns were positioned. During his reconnaissance, Maney saw Parsons' guns, as well as the 123rd Illinois Infantry Regiment, part of Terrill's brigade, which was posted to the right (south) of the guns. Realizing, however, that Donelson needed "immediate assistance," the general fell back to the depression to send his troops forward. Donelson's faltering attack, he wrote, "committed me to engagement without delay."[76]

Maney arranged his regiments into two lines. In the front line, the general placed the 9th Tennessee on the left, the 6th Tennessee in the center and the 41st Georgia—his inexperienced regiment—on the right. These three regiments, which totaled about 1,200 hundred men, Maney wrote, constituted "as much front as could be brought to bear advangeously [sic] against the Battery." He then ordered a staff officer to direct the 1st Tennessee and 27th Tennessee to create a second, reserve line, with the 1ˢᵗ Tennessee on the left and the 27ᵗʰ on the right. Together, these two regiments numbered about 600 men. Fearful of Donelson's imminent destruction, without waiting for his second line to organize, Maney ordered the first three regiments to advance on Parsons' battery. As the men surged forward, Captain John Curtwright of the 41ˢᵗ Georgia shouted to his green troops, "Keep cool, my boys! Keep cool! Shoot low!" For Maney's Brigade, the battle was about to begin.[77]

Chapter 5

"A Terrific and Deadly Fire"

The ground shook from Parsons' cannons as Maney's first line advanced through the woods. Because of the underbrush, the Federal troops on the ridge were unaware of Maney's movements. Union Captain Samuel Starling, on the ridge near Parsons' battery, wrote that "here the first disaster occurred. The enemy came creeping along through the woods their dress so of the color of grass, that you could hardly see them." The Rebels, primarily wearing butternut uniforms, blended in with the brown, drought-stricken woods. This accidental camouflage gave the Southerners an element of surprise. Federal officers and enlisted men alike, their attention diverted by Donelson's attack, were shocked to see Maney's troops moving toward the 123rd Illinois Infantry.[78]

Most of the Northern soldiers spotted Maney's advance when the brigade was easily within musket range. Union Captain Percival Oldershaw, the assistant adjutant general for Brigadier General James S. Jackson's 10th Division, remarked that the Unionists on the ridge first saw Maney's Brigade when they were only ninety yards away. Oldershaw wrote that "it was a great surprise to General Jackson [who was on the ridge near Parsons' guns] and myself…that the enemy was near to us."[79]

When the Rebels appeared, Terrill and Parsons, who were both directing the cannon fire against Donelson's Brigade, ordered the artillerymen to shift their aim from Donelson (to the south) to fire at Maney (to the east/northeast). As the Tennesseans and Georgians neared the split-rail fence, Parsons' battery fired into the woods, sending canister and shell into the

Rebel ranks. The men of the 123rd Illinois Infantry also emptied their muskets into the forest, hoping to stem the Southern assault. Lieutenant Colonel William Frierson of the 27th Tennessee noted, "During the whole time of passing through the woods the battery was playing on us with terrible effect." Maney's horse was shot out from under him, so the brigade commander advanced on foot.[80]

According to Colonel George Porter of the 6th Tennessee, Maney's Brigade had only moved "a short distance" through the woods when "one of the most deadly and destructive fires that can possibly be imagined was poured into their whole line by the enemy, who occupied a strong and well-chosen position in an open field about 300 yards to the front. Here [the enemy] had a battery of eight guns, strongly supported by infantry."[81]

Although it was about 2:30 p.m., only a portion of Union Brigadier General William R. Terrill's 33rd Brigade, which anchored the northern end of the Federals' defensive line, was on the ridge. Parsons' battery and the 123rd Illinois were the only Union units present when Maney began his assault, but more troops were rushing toward the sound of the fighting, including Terrill's 105th Ohio, the 80th Illinois and a detachment of 194 infantrymen commanded by Colonel Theophilus Garrard. Terrill's brigade was short one regiment—the 101st Indiana had been detached during the march to guard a train near Springfield—but all available troops were hustling toward Parsons' ridge.[82]

For the Confederates, Parsons' eight guns must have been a daunting sight. The Rebel infantry, however, did not know that most of the gunners were inexperienced. The battery had recently been organized in Louisville, and at least 100 of the 136 artillerymen were volunteers from the 105th Ohio Infantry. These men, raw troops with limited experience firing the pieces, manned three different types of guns, including five twelve-pounder bronze smoothbore Napoleons, two twelve-pounder bronze smoothbore field howitzers and one 2.9-inch Parrott rifle. Although the gunners were neophytes, Captain Henry Cummings, an Ohio infantryman who commanded a section of Parsons' guns, wrote, "We worked and drilled untiringly to get our battery into shape and learn to handle it." Terrill, a trained artilleryman, helped instruct the new gunners.[83]

The battery commander was tenacious. Charles Parsons was an Ohio native who had graduated from West Point barely one year before the Battle of Perryville. One Union officer wrote that he had seen Parsons

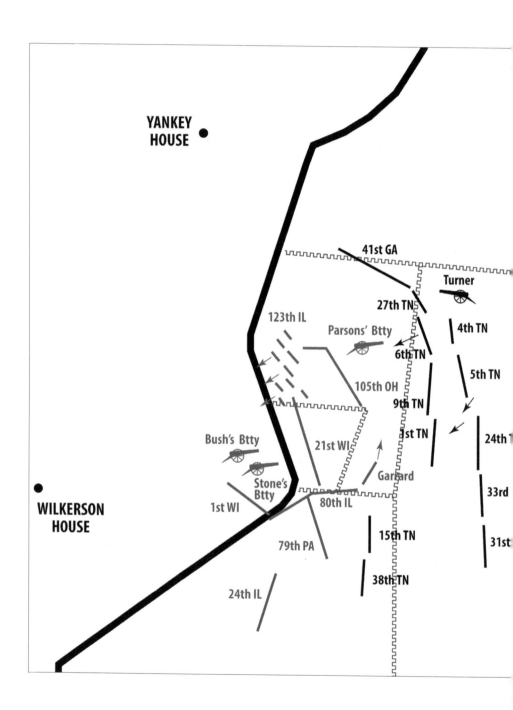

2:45 p.m.

WALKER HOUSE
●

KIRKLAND HOUSE
●

This map, based on maps created by Perryville park manager Kurt Holman, shows Maney's Brigade striking Union Brigadier General William R. Terrill's 33rd Brigade, which was posted on a hill now known as Parsons' ridge. This map depicts the action on the extreme Union left flank at about 2:45 p.m. *Map design courtesy of Charley Pallos.*

"knocked down seven times in a fight with a bigger man at West Point, without ever a thought of quitting so long as he could get up." Assigned to the artillery, Parsons took command of this improvised battery when Buell reorganized his force in Louisville.[84]

When the battery turned its eight guns on Maney's troops, the 41st Georgia bore the brunt of the artillery fire. Most of Maney's Brigade fronted the 123rd Illinois, so three of Parsons' guns were pointed at the Georgians on Maney's right wing. The cannon fire tore into the Peach State soldiers. Captain Oldershaw noted that the fire "checked the advance of the enemy, and after a few more rounds they changed front and faced the battery, which then flanked our left." According to Major John Knight of the 41st Georgia, his regiment was the first to be struck by the artillery. His troops, however, met the "terrific and deadly fire" with a volley of musketry. The Georgians' inexperience was evident. After firing, the regiment's advance stalled when the five hundred green troops attempted to reload their rifles under enemy fire for the first time.[85]

Maney explained that the 41st Georgia suffered severely because of the terrain. "From the nature of the ground the right of my line first emerged from the shelter of the ridge under which it had been formed and immediately the enemy's fire was opened upon it," he wrote. "Steadily and rapidly," however, the three lead regiments continued their advance through the woods.[86]

Maney's command reached the split-rail fence that divided the woods from the cleared hill. Artillery shells exploded in the treetops, and the Confederates instinctively halted behind the bramble-covered rails. Terrill panicked. According to one Union soldier, Terrill was obsessed with the safety of the artillery, and "its peril absorbed his whole attention." The Southern soldiers lined the fence, and the Virginia-born Union officer foolishly ordered the 123rd Illinois Infantry to make a bayonet charge against Maney's three regiments. Terrill hoped that his infantry could drive Maney's Brigade away from the fence, thereby saving his eight cannons. "Forward!" Terrill shouted. "Do not let them get the guns!" A Union soldier wrote that when the 123rd Illinois surged down the hill, Terrill "remained beside the battery, directing and encouraging [Parsons'] men in its operation." The bayonets of the Illinois troops flashed in the sun, and Terrill's "face flushed with agony at the thought of losing the battery of which he was so proud."[87]

The 123rd Illinois was a new regiment that had been organized at Mattoon, Illinois, and mustered into the army on September 6. The troops, in the service for barely a month, were armed primarily with .58-caliber Austrian rifled muskets, but about one man in seven carried a .58-caliber Springfield rifle. Most of the soldiers were from Cumberland, Clark, Crawford and Coles Counties, and with the exception of their commander, Colonel James Monroe, none of the regiment's officers or men had any military experience. In fact, the regiment had never practiced battalion drill, and only a few of the companies had participated in drill of any kind. During their few weeks in the military, their service had been confined to the construction of fortifications at Louisville. This new regiment's bayonet charge against Maney's command was marked with confusion and probably consisted of little more than an armed mob careening down the hill. When the 772 troops advanced, they did so with their rear rank in front. Terrill had sent lambs to the slaughter.[88]

The shouting Union regiment poured down the steep hill toward the fence. Oldershaw related that the raw Illinois troops "advanced bravely, but unfortunately the enemy had not left the woods, and there was a rail-fence on its edge, which prevented their doing so promptly." These new soldiers advanced against veteran Confederates, who could load and fire much faster. The Rebels held a further advantage because when the Union soldiers moved down the hill, historian Kenneth Hafendorfer wrote, "[b]y virtue of the sloping ground, Maney's men were able to deliver fire from consecutive battalions in the rear of each other."[89]

The Southern musketry shocked the green Federal troops. A.D. Cleaver of the 123rd Illinois commented, "We were ordered to fall down at the first fire of the rebels which we did. So heavy was the fire that we could see their bullets in the air." Major James A. Connolly recalled that "[m]ost of the bullets went over our heads and sounded like a swarm of bees running away in the hot summer air overhead."[90]

For the new troops, the fear of combat, their exhaustion from the march from Louisville and the drought compounded their suffering. Cleaver told his family that "I thought I had suffered for water in my time but—Oh, no one but a soldier knows what a thirst the steam from the hot blood, the dust, and the powder smoke will create." The 123rd Illinois neared the fence and fired one volley into the woods, but the massed fire from nearly 1,600 muskets blazing from consecutive battalions forced the Union troops back. These 772 men lost 36 killed, 118 wounded and 35 missing, a total of 24.5 percent of their force. Most of the casualties were incurred during the brief charge against the fence. Shaken, the bloodied Northerners fled back up the hill, past their initial position, and ran westward toward the rear.[91]

A modern view of Parsons' ridge, looking up the hill from Maney's position at the split-rail fence. At the time of the battle, eight Union cannons and Terrill's 33rd Brigade were posted on the ridge. *Courtesy of the author.*

Brigadier General James S. Jackson, commander of the Union 10th Division, was standing to the left of Parsons' guns, watching sheets of flame erupt from the Confederate position at the fence. Jackson, born in Fayette County, Kentucky, attended Centre College in nearby Danville before transferring to Jefferson College in Pennsylvania. Upon finishing his education, Jackson practiced law in Christian County, Kentucky. He served in the Mexican-American War but resigned his commission after dueling with a fellow officer. Known for participating in several affairs of honor, the hot-tempered Jackson served in the Kentucky legislature and became a prominent member of the Bluegrass State's Know-Nothing Party. Eventually elected to the U.S. Congress, he left his congressional seat when the Civil War erupted to raise the 3rd Kentucky Cavalry Regiment. The *New York Times* proclaimed, "In manner he was brusque and overbearing, and as a consequence was a party to numerous quarrels, which sometimes resulted in duels. One of the most notable of these difficulties was a street fight in Hopkinsville, Ky., in which he had the misfortune to kill his antagonist." In another antebellum duel, Jackson acted as a second to a man who dueled Lexington lawyer and politician Roger W. Hanson. During the Civil War, Jackson and Hanson again found themselves on opposite sides. Hanson led Kentucky's famed Confederate "Orphan Brigade" and was killed at the Battle of Stones River, Tennessee. Perryville was Jackson's first divisional command. His leadership would be brief.[92]

The night before the battle, seven miles from Perryville, Jackson and his brigade commanders, Terrill and Colonel George P. Webster, discussed the chances of an individual soldier being killed in battle. All agreed that troops would never be fearful, a Federal colonel later wrote, "if they considered the doctrine of probabilities and how slight the chance was of any particular person being killed. Theory failed, as it has often done before; all three were killed in the next day's fight." Jackson, Terrill and Webster all fell at Perryville, decimating the leadership of the 10th Division.[93]

Union Brigadier General James S. Jackson commanded the 10th Division at Perryville. Shortly after Maney's Brigade appeared at the base of Parson's ridge, Jackson was shot twice in the chest and killed. *Courtesy of the Kentucky Historical Society.*

When the 123rd Illinois raced back up the hill, Jackson was immediately shot twice in the right side of his chest. Captain Samuel Starling was standing twelve feet from Jackson when Maney's men emerged from the woods and reached the fence. Starling wrote that he and Jackson were both behind Parsons' cannons when "suddenly the minnie [sic] balls begun to pass us with their peculiar whizzing noise. Jackson & the rest of us were on foot holding our horses by their bridles, [when] he remarked, 'Well, I'll be damned if this is not getting rather particular.' In an instant he fell." Percival Oldershaw, Jackson's assistant adjutant general, ran up to the commander and "found him on his back struggling to speak, but unable to do so. He died in a few moments."[94]

In the same volley of Rebel gunfire, Jackson's black mare was also killed. Jackson, a proslavery Kentucky Unionist, had also brought an African American servant with him into the fray. Sadly, this slave was also killed during the fight.[95]

Starling and several aides ran up to the general and found him lying on his back. The captain wrote that Jackson's "eyes were closed…his mouth was open, and he gave several short spasmodic groans, but I am sure he breathed not once. There was a hole in his coat surrounded with blood ½ inch all around it, immediately below his right nipple." Starling added that "2 bullets had passed entirely through him one from the front and another from one side to the other, but not deep. the [sic] last would not have killed him."[96]

With bullets flying past, Starling and Oldershaw picked up Jackson's corpse and carried him one hundred yards down the back slope of the hill. Jackson, however, "was a heavy man," and Oldershaw, stricken with back problems, could not carry the general. The two officers put the body down and moved to the rear to procure an ambulance for Jackson's corpse. By the time they returned, however, the Rebels had taken the hill, and Jackson's body was within enemy lines.[97]

Despite the death of the division commander, Oldershaw admitted that Jackson's demise was not demoralizing for the troops. First, the soldiers were new recruits and had not grown attached to their commander. Second, many of the men, who were either fleeing or were prone at the time, did not see Jackson fall. He was the first general officer to be killed during the Battle of Perryville and was the highest-ranking officer to die. Another—who was Jackson's friend and immediate subordinate—would soon follow.[98]

The 9th Tennessee, 6th Tennessee and 41st Georgia emerged from the woods and halted at the rail fence, struck by musketry, artillery shells and

This 1885 photograph shows a tree located behind Parsons' ridge. According to local legend, shortly after Union Brigadier General James S. Jackson was killed, his body was dragged to this tree. The day after the battle, his remains were recovered and sent to Louisville for burial. He was later reinterred in his hometown of Hopkinsville, Kentucky. *Courtesy of the Perryville Battlefield State Historic Site.*

canister. Confederate artillery soon answered the Union guns. Captain William Turner's battery, attached to Maney's Brigade, unlimbered three hundred yards east of the fence and fired shells and canister onto Parsons' position. Although the Confederate infantry had repelled the 123rd Illinois's bayonet charge, it was difficult for officers to coax the men forward from behind the shelter of the rails. Colonel George Porter of the 6th Tennessee wrote, "[I]t seemed impossible for humanity to go farther, such was the havoc and destruction that had taken place in their ranks." Major John Knight of the 41st Georgia recalled that upon reaching the fence, the brigade "instinctively halted." Knight and the other Georgia officers attempted to rally the unit but failed. Bob Douglas of Company E waved his sword over his head and implored the troops to stand firm, while Frank McWhorter shouted, "Die my comrades, rather than give it up!"[99]

Maney realized the danger of halting at the fence. Parsons' eight guns poured fire on the men from less than 120 yards away and, he wrote, "together with his entire Infantry support concentrated a most terrific and deadly fire upon" the brigade. Although his three front regiments returned fire, Maney remarked, "This was unfavorable. The Enemy's Battery together with his entire infantry force (a full brigade) were pouring destruction upon us. Casting more shots and to better advantage than ourselves." The enemy fire, and his troops' stalled momentum at the fence, was a growing cause of concern.[100]

Chapter 6

"A Rain of Lead"

M aney's subordinates were frustrated that the attack had stalled. Lieutenant James I. Hall of the 9th Tennessee, who, like the slain General Jackson, had attended Centre College, recalled, "I remember that our advance up the hill was hindered by a worm fence, the corners of which were grown up thick with brushes and briars. This fence had to be let down in some places to enable our officers to ride through."[101]

Casualties mounted as the Southerners lost momentum. In the 9th Tennessee, which was on the left of Maney's first line, Colonel John W. Buford was critically wounded and taken to the rear. Command devolved on Major George W. Kelsoe. When Kelsoe took command, he rode through a gap in the fence, and his horse was shot. Lieutenant Hall later wrote, "It was a very valuable horse [which] had cost him five hundred dollars a few days before and Kelso [*sic*] thought it would be prudent for him to take the horse to the rear for treatment. This left us without Regimental officers." With his horse wounded and bullets literally buzzing in the October air, Kelsoe was likely more worried about his own health. Hall added that at the fence, "We lost a good many men here." Kelsoe did not want to become another one of those casualties.[102]

The barrage was also severe for Maney's reserve line. Lieutenant Colonel William Frierson of the 27th Tennessee, whose regiment was beginning to intermingle with the first line, noted that "as soon as the fence was reached, in full view of the battery, such a storm of shell, grape, canister, and Minie balls was turned loose upon us as no troops scarcely ever before encountered. Large

A modern view looking east from Parsons' ridge toward the split-rail fence where Maney's Brigade initially halted. Union Captain Charles Parsons's eight cannons and Terrill's infantry were posted on this hill. Union Brigadier General James S. Jackson was killed near this location. *Courtesy of the author.*

boughs were torn from the trees, the trees themselves shattered as if by lightning, and the ground plowed in deep furrows."[103]

Although the 123rd Illinois had raced to the rear, the Confederates still faced Parsons' battery and another large Federal regiment. When Donelson's attack commenced, Terrill ordered the 105th Ohio Infantry to form to the left of Parsons' guns. The men arrived on the field both as the 123rd Illinois was driven from the fence and as Jackson fell dead. Commanded by Colonel Albert Hall, the 105th Ohio was a new regiment of 645 men. Organized in Cleveland, these Buckeyes mustered into service on August 20, 1862, less than two months before the battle. Armed with Model 1861 .58-caliber Springfield rifles, this regiment was so new that it had no regimental banner. In fact, the 105th borrowed the colors of the 101st Indiana, the unit that was guarding the train in Springfield.[104]

When the Ohioans rushed toward the fighting, Private Josiah Ayre of Company E could hear the musketry crackling. Their pace quickened, and

Ira Nye of Company F told his friends goodbye, for he knew "that his time had come." Perryville provided a shocking baptism of fire for the 105th Ohio. Ayre wrote, "[A]s we neared the battle ground we saw the wounded coming [off]…this was a new sight to us [as] we reached the open field where the fighting was." The prophetic Nye was soon shot in the chest and killed.[105]

Approaching the back (western) side of Parsons' ridge, Albion Tourgee of the 105th Ohio's Company G saw his first battle. "On a little knoll to our right front," he wrote, "the battery was firing with frenzied rapidity. The shells from the enemy's battery flew over our heads and cut the limbs off the trees by which we stood, sending down a shower of acorns. Bullets pattered about us. We could see the artillerymen dashing back and forth as the smoke lifted from the guns. Men [members of the 123rd Illinois] were coming back from the hill which the crest hid from our view, some wounded, some stragglers." Tourgee added that at least half of Parsons' guns were inactive because of casualties, and men and horses were falling as the regiment approached. Another soldier simply remarked that the battery was "deserted." Ohioan Charles Radcliffe wrote that the troops were met with a "tornado of lead and iron sweeping that knoll" and that Jackson was "lying dead near the guns."[106]

Upon reaching the crest of the ridge, the green Buckeyes formed behind and to the left of Parsons' artillery. Terrill, completely engrossed with his cannons, had one of his staff officers place the regiment into position. Tourgee was not surprised with his brigade commander's obsession with the guns. "He was by training," the lieutenant wrote, "almost by instinct, an artilleryman, and his battery's action eclipsed [any] interest [in] the maneuvering of his brigade." Terrill, commanding an infantry brigade for the first time, made a terrible mistake. Instead of leaving the direction of the battery to the tenacious Parsons, Terrill ignored the action unfolding around him and instead focused on his prized artillery. Tourgee recognized the error. He wrote that the Virginian "had been so absorbed in the working of the guns that he had little idea of the severity of the attack."[107]

Terrill's undivided attention, however, would not have lessened the confusion that erupted when the 105th Ohio took its position. The regiment marched up to the cannons in column and then faced to the west, away from the attack. It is likely that the inexperienced officers were trying to ensure the unit's cohesiveness. When members of the regiment were struck in the back by gunfire, their commander, Colonel Albert Hall, yelled "about face," and the troops turned toward the enemy. Thus, the regiment lined up on the crest, with the left wing of the regiment on the right side of the line and the rear rank in front. Private Ayre remarked that they "could not form into a proper line and

Private William Howard, Company K, 105th Ohio, was killed in action during the Battle of Perryville. *Courtesy of the Perryville Battlefield State Historic Site.*

after going through several maneuvers in order to do so we became mixed and confused." With Parsons' cannons booming a few yards away, many of the men could not hear their officers' commands. Finally, however, the Ohioans formed a jumbled line on the hill. As the regiment deployed on the extreme Federal left, it refused, or bent back, its left side to protect that flank.[108]

The sight of Maney's Confederates was a shock to the new troops. Tourgee remarked that when the regiment formed on the hill, "There we first saw the enemy, two lines of gray in the edge of the brown woods scarcely ninety yards away. Puffs of smoke and jets of flame shot out from the undergrowth and along the fence." For members of this regiment, the sharply sloping ground on that side of the hill made it difficult to see the enemy. Furthermore, the speed with which the veteran Confederates fired placed the Buckeyes at a disadvantage. Private Bliss Morse commented, "[T]he rebels had the start of us by two rounds while we were forming and loading our pieces."[109]

The Confederate fire dropped several members of the 105th Ohio, including one exceptionally dedicated soldier. Elbridge Early was a member of Company K who was sick in a Lexington hospital when Kirby Smith's Rebels took that city. Early, suffering from a severe fever, crawled off his cot, escaped town and traveled more than one hundred miles to rejoin his regiment in Louisville. Still horribly ill, Early marched with his comrades to Perryville. During the fight on the ridge, Early was standing in the front line. Shot in the hip, he continued the struggle until a bullet in the temple brought him down.[110]

Despite the confusion at the top of the hill, Maney's men—with the shells exploding in the branches, the canister balls smashing into trees and bullets pattering off the fence rails—remained pinned down. Cheatham, watching the attack stall, personally directed the fire of Turner's Battery from its position on a slight ridge three hundred yards east of the fence. Organized in July 1861, Turner's gunners were from Quitman, Tunica, Clark and Coahoma Counties in Mississippi. The men had been in the service for sixteen months, and the fires of Belmont and Shiloh had forged them into veterans. Under Cheatham's direction, the battery positioned its two twelve-pounder bronze smoothbores and two six-pounder smoothbore cannons on the ridge.[111]

Maney's adjutant, Thomas Malone, remarked that while the brigade was caught at the fence, Turner's accuracy saved the command. "It seemed to me that our men could not have maintained our position at all but for the fact that old Turner—the best artilleryman, but the poorest drilled man in the army—was imperatively demanding the attention of Parson's [sic] guns," Malone wrote. "He thundered with his little 6-pound howitzers right over the heads of our men, and with grape was making it very hot for Parsons and his infantry supports."[112]

W.H. Smith, a member of Turner's Battery, was blasting away at the Union gunners when he heard someone shout, "Let me try my hand at them." Turning around, Smith saw Cheatham standing by the guns. "I stood aside," Smith recalled, "and he fired several rounds, pointing the gun and directing the fire apparently with as much pleasure as a boy shooting at rabbits."[113]

Several of the gunners displayed courage that day. At one point, a shell exploded over the limber chest of one of the guns. The packing around the powder caught fire and threatened to explode. One of the artillerymen, calmly going about his duty, pulled the flaming packing out of the chest. Without pausing, he resumed his service preparing ammunition for the gun crew.[114]

While the Confederate attack ground down at the fence, the remainder of Terrill's brigade reached the field. It was about 3:15 p.m., and the fight on the Union left had been raging for about forty-five minutes. The 659 men of Colonel

Maney's Brigade was part of Confederate Major General Benjamin F. Cheatham's division. *Courtesy of the Library of Congress.*

Thomas G. Allen's 80th Illinois Infantry and the small 194-man detachment led by Colonel Theophilus T. Garrard reached the back slope of Parsons' ridge. The men fixed bayonets and moved westward, toward the fighting.[115]

Like most of Terrill's units, Allen's 80th Illinois was a green regiment. Organized that August in Centralia, Illinois, the regiment was recruited from Plains, Madison, St. Clair, Washington, Jefferson, Marion, Randolph and Perry Counties. Handed their .58-caliber Model 1861 Springfield rifles, the men were sent to Louisville and joined the Army of the Ohio on September 4. One Illinois native noted that "Perryville was a quick and brutal initiation of new Illinois regiments to warfare. For some soldiers, just weeks away from home, it had all happened too suddenly."[116]

Garrard's 194 men also discovered the brutality of Perryville. The battalion-sized detachment was composed of men from the 7th Kentucky, 32nd Kentucky and 3rd Tennessee Infantry Regiments. Many of the men were survivors of the Battle of Richmond, but all were essentially raw recruits. Their commander, the fifty-year-old Theophilus Garrard, was the grandson of a Kentucky governor. Born near Manchester, Kentucky, Garrard sat in the state legislature before serving in the Mexican-American War. Although Garrard traveled to California to partake in the gold rush, this unsuccessful miner returned to his native state and raised an infantry regiment. One Federal officer noted that Garrard was "a strong, plain, firm man, who had his convictions of right and wrong and stood by them; a farmer born in the mountains…[he was] a staunch Union man as the oaks on his native hills."[117]

Armed with Enfield rifles, seventy-five men of the 7th Kentucky joined Garrard immediately before Perryville. Organized at Camp Dick Robinson as the 3rd Kentucky, the outfit was renamed the 7th Kentucky because other regiments in the state had been given the same designation. The men, most of whom were from the mountains of eastern Kentucky, refused to accept the change of moniker and continued to call themselves the 3rd Kentucky. They fought at Camp Wildcat near London, Kentucky, and helped capture Cumberland Gap in June 1862. Besieged at the Gap when Kirby Smith invaded the commonwealth, these men escaped to Lexington, where they were scattered at the Battle of Richmond. Eventually reaching Louisville, the survivors joined Garrard's detachment. They were among the few veterans in Terrill's command.[118]

The 32nd Kentucky, numbering forty-five men, was organized in response to the Confederate invasion of the state. Distributed Model 1816 conversion muskets, these men entered the service in Frankfort in early August and were commanded by Captain Robert Taylor, a Frankfort native. The final

Left: Union Colonel Theophilus Garrard, the grandson of a Kentucky governor, commanded a 194-man detachment at the Battle of Perryville. A native of Manchester, Kentucky, Garrard was a former state legislator and veteran of the Mexican-American War. *Courtesy of the Library of Congress.*

Below: This 1885 image of the Perryville battlefield shows one of the many tall rail fences that would have been found on the field during the battle. During the early stages of the action, Maney's Brigade halted behind a split-rail fence at the base of Parsons' ridge as it battled Union troops commanded by Brigadier General William Terrill. Maney's Brigade suffered heavily while it was halted at the fence. *Courtesy of the Perryville Battlefield State Historic Site.*

members of the detachment, the Enfield-wielding 3rd Tennessee Union Infantry, battled fellow Tennesseans at Perryville.[119]

Garrard's detachment and the 80th Illinois reached the crest of the hill and formed battle lines amid intense gunfire. While the 105th Ohio stumbled to the left of Parsons' guns with its flank refused (bent back), Garrard's detachment took position on the right side of the Union artillery. To its right, the 80th Illinois stretched its battle lines farther to the south. Its line snaked down the gentle southern slope of the ridge.[120]

With more Union troops deploying, Maney feared that his brigade's failed momentum would lead to disaster. Finding his adjutant, Thomas Malone, both officers conferred near the fence under a white oak tree. Both agreed that it was too dangerous to retreat. With his troops pinned down, Maney knew that he had one chance to advance, crush Terrill's infantry and take the battery. In addition, Maney knew that a retreat would leave Donelson's Brigade unsupported. Furthermore, with all of Parsons' guns aimed at his Tennesseans and Georgians, a retreat through the woods would be deadly. Malone informed Maney that the three Confederate regiments could take the ridge. "Go," Maney ordered, "direct the men to go forward, if possible."[121]

Amid the roar of musketry and cannons, Malone mounted his horse and rode up and down the line, telling the troops to prepare to leap the fence and charge the hill. Maney, still on foot after his horse had been shot, also moved down the line, urging the men forward. When the general passed the 6th Tennessee at the center of the Confederate line, Malone rode his mount "three horse lengths in front" of the fence and raised his hat to signal the charge. "Every man was instantly on his feet," Malone wrote, "and I don't suppose that twelve hundred men ever gave such a yell before."[122]

When the Confederates rose to charge, some officers viewed the dead and wounded men who were sprawled at the base of the fence. "It was a fearful time," recalled Major Knight of the 41st Georgia. "At this critical moment General Maney passed down our line, encouraging the men by his personal presence, and urging them forward. Just at this place our regiment sustained one-half if not two-thirds, of their entire loss during the battle." For the lead regiments in Maney's line, the halt at the fence caused significant losses.[123]

The three front regiments leapt to their feet, climbed the fence and charged up the ridge. John Morse of the 105th Ohio wrote, "There was a gully between us and the enemy full of bushes. We delivered our fire on the enemy in the edge of the woods and in a moment the gully was alive with the enemy who arose from the bushes and at the same time advanced from the woods, firing as they came, and opened on us from a battery with grape and canister." Tourgee also recalled the chilling Confederate advance. "Then we first heard the rebel yell we were to hear so often afterwards," he wrote. "The gray line burst from the wood and rushed up the slope." At this moment, he added, "The air was full of flashing ramrods."[124]

Terrill's green infantrymen responded to the advance with gunfire. One member of the 41st Georgia, whose regiment incurred the brunt of Parsons' fire, recalled the danger of crossing the fence. He wrote that when the unit was "within one hundred and fifty yards of the enemy, they opened on us with grape and canister. When within fifty yards, they opened on us with musketry, and now the fight became general and looked like the whole world had been converted into blue coats, whistling balls, bursting shells and brass cannon. Right here it was almost impossible for mortal men to stand up in the face of such a rain of lead."[125]

Ohioan John Morse felt this storm. When bullets showered on his regiment "as thick as hail," one ball and one piece of buckshot struck his rifle butt. Another bullet shot through a blanket that was coiled over his shoulder, and another spent buckshot bruised his knee. Just as the 123rd Illinois endured fire from consecutive battalions in rear of one another, so, too, did the 105th Ohio. When the Confederates moved up the slope and fired uphill, men in the rear ranks let loose accurate shots at the bluecoats on the crest of the ridge. The green Ohioans managed to fire three volleys before falling back.[126]

"The brave men seemed only to need know what was desired," Maney reported, "and though many had fallen during the unfortunate short halt at the fence, the survivors dashed forward seemingly reckless of the danger and death before them." Few Confederates were as bold as the regimental color-bearers. Joe Wheeler, Company I, 27th Tennessee Infantry, held his regimental banner. While carrying the flag up the hill, Wheeler's right arm was "shattered" by Federal fire. Seizing the flag with his left hand, Wheeler continued to hold the colors aloft until he was shot in the head and killed. The bullets were also dangerous for the bearers of the 6th Tennessee, who held the center of Maney's line. After two color-bearers were shot down, Private A.M. Pegues grasped the flag. During the struggle near the fence, Pegues was "shot in three places."[127]

Maney's advance was thrilling for one observer: General Frank Cheatham. The division commander wrote:

I had placed myself about one hundred yards to the right of Maney's brigade and on a line with them, where I could look down the lines between the contending forces…I could see in the smoke occasionally that as his men fired they would take one step forward to load, which assured me they were making progress under that terrible storm of artillery and musketry. To me it was the most exciting few moments of my life.[128]

During the charge up the ridge, Malone stumbled across the body of Brigadier General James S. Jackson. Malone found the Kentuckian "lying on his back, with his feet toward the front, as gallant looking a soldier as I ever saw." Malone stopped to snip off one of Jackson's buttons as a souvenir, which he later gave to his sister. Fellow Tennessean Emmett Cockrill approached and said, "Why, damn it! that's [sic] Jim Jackson!" The two men had been friends prior to the war. Staring at the deceased officer, Cockrill muttered, "Well, Jim, old boy, you ought to have had better luck!" Malone later noted that this "was all Emmitt [sic] had to say. It strikes one now as very unfeeling, but at the time it seemed to me all right."[129]

Maney was pleased with his troops' advance. The brigade commander stayed with his first line until it neared Parsons' battery and drove off most of the inexperienced gunners. After spending time finding a horse, Maney remounted and turned to look for his second line. Almost as soon as his feet were in the stirrups, he was relieved to see the 1st Tennessee advancing toward the fence.

Thankful that his second line had arrived intact, the brigade commander checked the progress of his first three regiments. When his eyes swept past the carnage around the fence and the men who had fallen in heaps up the slope, panic struck. "I observed to my great surprise and anxiety," he reported, "my front line halted about one hundred yards in advance of me and within perhaps forty yards of the Battery lying on the ground and hotly engaged and firing against the Enemy's Battery support which was protected by the crest of the hill." Although the men were less than one hundred feet away from Parsons' guns, instead of continuing the advance, Maney's command fell prone and peppered the Union soldiers with musketry.[130]

The Unionists on Parsons' ridge also fell prone, and Malone was surprised that a significant number of enemy soldiers were hit. "But what struck me at the time and strikes me now," he wrote, "is the fatal accuracy of the fire of the 41st, 6th, and 9th while the enemy were lying down. It seemed to me that one-third of them were lying dead on the line which they had been holding so gallantly." Despite the accurate fire, Maney's attack had again stalled.[131]

Chapter 7

"BREAK THE ENEMY BEFORE THEM"

For the second time, Brigadier General George Maney's attack had lost momentum. As Parsons' artillerymen and the 105th Ohio fired down the hill, the Confederates lay down halfway up the slope and returned fire. This delay changed Maney's plan of keeping two regiments in reserve while the first three carried the Union position. While Maney's lead regiments were pinned down near the guns, the 27th Tennessee crossed the fence and caught up with the first line. Eager to enter the bout, these Tennesseans squeezed between the 6th Tennessee and the 41st Georgia, plugging a gap that had emerged during the charge. Now, a four-regiment front faced the remnants of Parsons' artillery and Terrill's infantry, with the 9th Tennessee on the left, the 6th Tennessee on the left-center, the 27th Tennessee on the right-center and the 41st Georgia on the far right. The 1st Tennessee only remained in reserve because an officer (possibly Maney) halted it near the fence.[132]

Although the Union troops had been bloodied, their fire checked the Confederates. Lieutenant James Hall of the 9th Tennessee recalled that "[a]t this point in our advance, we were brought under the fire of the battery not fifty feet in front of us and of the infantry line in its rear. Their fire was terrific and we were losing men rapidly; so much so that it caused our line to falter its advance." The other regiments were also battered. Colonel George Porter of the 6th Tennessee said that his regiment suffered its heaviest casualties during the advance up the hill. This proved to be "the hottest part of the engagement." With the men caught on an open hill less than one hundred feet from eight cannons and hundreds of infantrymen, it is no wonder.[133]

Frankfort native Captain Robert Taylor commanded forty-five members of the 32nd Kentucky (Union) Infantry at the Battle of Perryville. Taylor's men were part of Colonel T.T. Garrard's detachment, which battled Maney's Brigade in the area around Parsons' ridge. After the battle, Taylor helped remove wounded soldiers from the battleground. *Courtesy of the Kentucky Historical Society.*

Although the Rebels were pinned down, their counter fire proved deadly to the Union defenders. As the Southerners advanced, one Confederate remarked that "it looked as if [our lines] were a solid sheet of flame." Captain Robert Taylor of Garrard's detachment noted that his command "endured a fearful storm of balls, round shot, and bursting shell for half an hour."[134]

Maney, with the 1st Tennessee near the split-rail fence, watched his first line halt halfway up the hill. Although he saw junior officers try to rally the men, the brigade commander found that the noise of combat made the pleas fall on deaf ears. He worried that his attack would fail. "The Enemy in front greatly outnumbered my command, besides his battery," he reported. "To recoil before such a force unless properly covered and redeemed was ruin." The brigade was again in a precarious position. "The danger," he recalled, "seemed imminent," but he realized that "to hold the field the capture [of] the battery was a necessity." Therefore, he considered sending his reserve up the hill to take the artillery.[135]

Maney was later criticized for not personally leading the charge up the hill. Several of his subordinate officers expressed regret that their commander had been with the reserve line during this critical moment. When these officers questioned Maney's actions, he responded in his October 26 report that "[m]y knowledge of the field, the location of the enemy, the disposition of our own troops and, to an extent of our own plan of action [it] was necessary for advantageous management of my reserve and rendered my personal presence with it indispensable until my information and instructions on these particulars could be imparted." In brief, Maney argued that since he had scouted the field, he knew what was best for the reserve. Moreover, at Perryville, Maney was injured when he was kicked in the head by his horse (possibly when remounting after his own horse was shot out from under him). This may have also hindered his ability to advance with his first line, and he may have remained at the fence in order to regain his senses.[136]

Maney added that he stayed with the reserve in case his first line crumbled from the stalled assault. If his front regiments were pushed back, the general argued, he would be near the fence to assume command amid the chaos. Maney's defense of his actions were later bolstered when Cheatham said that Maney "was by my side" during the attack. Since the division commander did not complain about Maney's actions, subordinate voices were hushed. Months after the battle, however, Maney fought a duel to defend his honor against charges that he did not do his duty at Perryville.[137]

With his advanced stalled, Maney gave instructions to Colonel Hume Feild of the 1st Tennessee Infantry. The general's staff officers were still absent on other assignments, and Maney was insistent on staying with his reserve in case his front regiments broke. Therefore, Maney told Feild to move forward, take command of the front line and renew the attack. Feild was to instruct the regimental commanders "to make [a] concerted and all possible effort to carry their line over the hill top and break the enemy before them." Maney would remain with the reserve in order to keep control over the entire brigade. Once Feild left his regiment and moved up the slope, command of the 1st Tennessee devolved on Lieutenant Colonel John Patterson.[138]

Maney had picked the best man for the job. An 1856 graduate of the Kentucky Military Institute, Feild initially opposed secession. However, he said, "When the first gun boomed at Fort Sumter, the die was cast; then I was heart and soul with the South." Feild organized an infantry company in Giles County, Tennessee, and was named captain, and the unit joined the

1st Tennessee. When Maney was promoted after the Battle of Shiloh, Feild replaced Maney as leader of the regiment.[139]

A few moments later, as the brigadier told Lieutenant Colonel Patterson what to do if the regiments were forced back, the officers were joined by Thomas Malone, Maney's adjutant. Maney promptly sent Malone to the front to order the attack to continue. Malone was one of the officers who later complained about Maney's absence from the ridge.[140]

After conferring with Patterson, Maney turned to find the 27th Tennessee Infantry, his other reserve regiment that was initially to the right of the 1st Tennessee. Much to his dismay, Maney discovered that the 27th had moved up the hill and joined his three lead regiments. When he found that these troops had piled in between the 6th Tennessee and the 41st Georgia, he was relieved. The 6th Tennessee and the 41st Georgia "had suffered severely by the destructive fire at the fence," so Maney was thankful that these two regiments had been reinforced, albeit accidentally.[141]

Upon learning that the 27th Tennessee had rushed forward, Maney finally moved to the front. As he walked up the hill, the men of his first line jumped to their feet and advanced. Apparently, Feild and Malone had been successful in rallying the troops. Maney reported that Malone, at the front of the Confederate line, urged the 9th Tennessee to attack Parsons' artillery. Malone, Maney recalled, "was followed by the 9th with a cheer [and] the other Regts [joined] promptly and gallantly in the movement."[142]

The brigade had rallied for a second, crucial time. Cheatham, still watching Maney's attack unfold, saw more Union troops moving toward the ridge. He wrote that he watched "a long line of the enemy's infantry moving by the left flank out of a ravine in rear of the enemy's artillery, for the purpose of flanking my men." Cheatham called for his artillery, and Turner's Battery moved forward and fired canister into this column while Maney' men continued the assault. Turner also trained his guns on two other Union batteries, located three hundred yards to the west of Parsons' position.[143]

The severity of the struggle up Parsons' ridge was revealed by the actions of a sixteen-year-old drummer boy from the 9th Tennessee. As the lad tapped out a cadence on his drum, a shell fragment destroyed his instrument. Without pausing, the boy picked up an abandoned musket and joined the fight. Using the butt of the rifle, the sixteen-year-old "crushed the skull of an artilleryman who was in the act of firing his gun." When asked why he took part in the carnage, the boy simply replied, "[W]hen they fout, I fit." Hundreds of Maney's men followed the same maxim.[144]

The Confederates cheered and charged up the slope toward Parsons' guns. Many of the Southerners held their fire until they drove the Federals back at the point of the bayonet. For Ohioan Charles Radcliffe, "It was useless to stay there and be annihilated." Malone recalled that once the Federal troops fled down the back side of the hill, the Rebels opened fire. He wrote that "shooting deliberately, the butchery was something awful. I remember stating at the time that I could walk upon dead bodies from where the enemy's line was established until it reached the woods, some three hundred yards away." Colonel George C. Porter of the 6th Tennessee added that the Northerners were driven off "with terrible slaughter."[145]

As the Union artillerymen and infantry fled from the hill, Turner concentrated his fire on two Federal batteries posted on a ridge three hundred yards west of Parsons' position. During the fight, Turner wrote, these two batteries "had annoyed us considerably, opening upon us with guns of heavier caliber than ours as soon as we commenced our firing." In addition, Turner blasted the retreating Union ranks with shells and spherical case shot. This allowed Maney's adjutant to comment that the Confederates "suffered terribly while we were charging, but the enemy still more after they had begun to run."[146]

At least one Federal officer refused to leave his post. Like the captain of a sinking ship, Charles Parsons, the unyielding Federal artilleryman, stood tall when his men left in the face of the Confederate onslaught. One Union officer remarked that Parsons had to be physically dragged from his guns. Most of the battery's horses had been killed, so the Federal gunners saved only one cannon, four caissons and two limbers. The remainder of the artillery, which had given Maney's Brigade so much trouble, was captured.[147]

The ordnance-strapped Confederates were joyous to seize these badly needed pieces. W.H. Smith, a veteran of Turner's Battery, commented that "[a]t Perryville we were given two more twelve-pound Napoleons captured from the enemy, giving us a complete battery of four Napoleons. Not having sufficient horses to haul off our old inferior guns, we cut them down and threw them into an old well near the battlefield." A reporter from the *New York Times* related that the Confederates spiked the remaining guns and hacked the carriage wheels to pieces.[148]

The Southern artillerymen were not the only Confederates to procure souvenirs on Parsons' ridge. One member of the 9th Tennessee, Lieutenant W.M. Cunningham, chose his own battlefield relic when his regiment swept past Parsons' silent guns. Cunningham picked up a silver spoon from an artillery caisson and kept the utensil for the remainder of his life.[149]

Parsons' 136 men lost 10 killed, 19 wounded and 10 missing, or 28.7 percent of their force. In addition, about fifty of the battery's horses were killed, which allowed the cannons to fall into Rebel hands. Parsons was crestfallen over the loss. Captain Oldershaw of the 10th Division saw the young officer as he moved to the rear. Oldershaw said that Parsons "appeared perfectly unmanned and broken-hearted." The artilleryman told his fellow officer that "I could not help it, captain; it was not my fault."[150]

Parsons was dejected, and Maney was overjoyed. He called the capture of the battery "one of the most desperate undertakings ending in perfect success of the war." Lieutenant Colonel William Frierson of the 27th Tennessee concurred. "It was a complete triumph of resolute courage and determined fighting over every odds."[151]

The success came at a great cost, and many of Maney's company and regimental commanders were killed, wounded or knocked out of the action. Immediately after Frierson watched the 27th Tennessee take the ridge, a Union artillery shell exploded near his head. Although he was not visibly wounded, the blast left him "incapacitated" for the remainder of the battle. As the Confederates followed the fleeing bluecoats down the back slope of the ridge, Lieutenant James Hall of the 9th Tennessee was shot through the torso. Two of Hall's comrades, who were most likely his former students, picked up the schoolteacher turned soldier and carried him to a shade tree. Although they were in the rear, the 1st Tennessee, Maney's reserve unit, also lost a handful of men when the ridge was taken.[152]

When Maney's command overran Parsons' position, Colonel Theophilus Garrard's Union detachment, located to the right of the guns, also fell back to the rear slope of the hill. At the same time, the 80th Illinois Infantry endured attacks from Confederate Brigadier General A.P. Stewart's brigade, namely the 4th and 5th Tennessee Infantry Regiments. In order to support Donelson and Maney's attacks, and to plug a gap that existed between these two brigades, Cheatham had ordered Stewart's troops to attack.[153]

Maney moved to the top of the ridge and surveyed the scene. Although the Union infantry had been driven back, some of Terrill's survivors were forming near the Benton Road, a fence-lined lane that ran about 250 yards behind Parsons' ridge. These Union soldiers numbered nearly two hundred men of the 105th Ohio and a handful of others from the 123rd Illinois and Garrard's detachment. Ohioan John Morse related that this was a tenuous position. "The shell, round shot, and bullets were constantly screaming and whirling around us and over our heads," he recalled.[154]

Morse's commander, Colonel Albert Hall of the 105th Ohio, noted that the fire from Turner's Battery and Maney's charge had made their position on the ridge so "untenable" that they were ordered away. Hall moved his command sixty yards down the back slope of the hill, toward the Benton Road. He then formed his regiment "on the line of an old fence, then much broken down. The enemy followed the movement, and when he reached the crest (our former position) received a fire that opened their ranks with the wildest havoc." Maney's momentum would not be checked by this hastily formed line. When the Rebels continued to move westward, the Union soldiers, still under fire from Turner's Battery, again fell back.

Terrill's troops retreated through a cornfield that grew immediately east of the Benton Road. Upon entering the field, one soldier wrote, "[T]he enemy followed sharply and their bullets cut stalk and leaf and rattled the kernels from the drooping ears beside us, every now and then claiming a victim." A majority of the 105th Ohio fled more than two hundred yards to the rear. Three of the companies, however, did not hear the order to retreat. These troops eventually fell back farther to the left "behind a stone fence that marked the roadway."[155]

Private Josiah Ayre was one of these Buckeyes. As he ran westward toward a ridge west of the Benton Road where Union Colonel John Starkweather had positioned his brigade, Ayre was shot, he wrote, "in my left leg just below the calf breaking it and passing clear through." Ayre fell, and within seconds, Maney's troops swarmed around him. One of the Confederates cut off Ayre's cartridge box and pressed on, continuing the attack. Lying on the ground, Ayre wrote, "the shot and shell flew thick over my head as I lay there making it very unsafe." Fearful, the Ohioan crawled behind a tree. About twenty-four hours later, he was found lying on the battlefield and was taken to a field hospital, where his wound was dressed. On October 11, 1862, Ayre ended his diary entry with the phrase, "all together I think my self lucky." His luck, however, did not hold. Ayre died three days later from complications to his leg wound.[156]

Albin Tourgee of the 105th Ohio believed that Terrill's fixation on the lost guns had led to the rout. He wrote that after most of the Union soldiers fell back behind Starkweather's position, Terrill "was very depressed, thinking not of what his men had done, but of what he had failed to accomplish." It's likely that Parsons, who said that it was not his fault, also blamed Terrill for the loss.[157]

From the top of Parsons' ridge, Maney could see his first line advance against the retreating foe. He reported, "My conclusion at this moment was [that] the Enemy['s] entire force at hand had been concentrated for the protection of the battery from which he had just been driven and that vigorous pressing even with one strong and spirited Regt. might do much toward his rout." The brigade commander again moved to the rear to bring up the 1st Tennessee. As he neared the fence, he met Lieutenant Colonel Patterson, now commanding the 1st, who informed him that General Polk had ordered the regiment to take Starkweather's batteries, which were posted on the ridge west of the Benton Road. Within minutes, Cheatham rode up and ordered Maney to take Starkweather's position. For the rest of the day Maney's command attacked Starkweather's troops.[158]

Chapter 8

THE CORNFIELD

A fter ordering Patterson and the 1st Tennessee forward, Maney joined his first line, which was barreling toward the cornfield located between Parsons' ridge and Starkweather's hill. There, Maney saw Stewart's Brigade advancing on his left. The Tennessean recalled that Stewart's presence "strengthened my confidence that the disordered condition of the enemy might be turned to a rout." When Maney reached his first line, however, he discovered his troops to be "greatly disordered." The commander, however, pushed these exhausted troops to continue their attack in order to keep pressure on the enemy as the 1st Tennessee entered the fray.[159]

Before Maney's Confederates reached Starkweather's position west of the Benton Road, they had to cross the cornfield located in the ravine between Parsons' ridge and Starkweather's hill. There, on the hill west of the road, was the bulk of John C. Starkweather's brigade, 2,500 soldiers from Illinois, Pennsylvania and Wisconsin. Twelve Union cannons, manned by Kentuckians and Hoosiers, were lined across the narrow ridge. The Benton Road coiled around the base of Starkweather's hill, and a rail and rock fence separated the cornfield from the lane. Standing amid the stalks of corn, nervously clutching their rifles, were the members of the 21st Wisconsin Infantry, one of Starkweather's regiments. There was little room for all of Starkweather's infantry on the ridge, so the 21st Wisconsin, the last of Starkweather's regiments to arrive on the field, was placed in front of the command. The 21st was a neophyte outfit, inexperienced and poorly positioned on the battlefield. Not only was Perryville its first battle, but also the regiment had only held battalion drill three times. Many of these soldiers had been in the service for less than a month. One veteran recalled that the troops "were absolutely without any experience, and could not obey commands from not knowing what they imported." Sadly, most of these Wisconsinites had never before fired their weapons.[160]

Armed with Austrian muskets, the 21st was so new that it carried no regimental flag. In fact, the march from Louisville proved that its troops were not hardened veterans. Although they mustered 1,006 men, nearly 600 fell out during the arduous trek to Perryville. By the time they were "placed in a corn field on a hill between our battery and the enemy," one soldier wrote, two of the regiment's companies (B and C) had left to scout after Rebel cavalry. Thus, the regiment was understrength and probably had little more than 400 men in the corn.[161]

The morning of the battle, the commander of the 21st Wisconsin, Colonel Benjamin Sweet, fell ill. The sound of cannons rumbling in the distance and orders to move to the front, however, invigorated the officer, and he moved forward with his regiment. At 9:00 a.m., the soft echoes of artillery rolled toward the men like "distant thunder far [off] towards the East among the hills," one member recalled. In fact, many of these green troops believed the cannons to be thunder. They hoped, in drought-stricken Kentucky, that it would rain and would "settle the dust and give us pure water." This mistake, however, was soon apparent.[162]

Upon reaching the battlefield, the men were placed in the cornfield that bordered the Benton Road. There, they were ordered to lie down. When they reached the field, the fight was raging to their front as Maney's Confederates battled Terrill's brigade for supremacy of Parsons' ridge. Michael Fitch of the 21st Wisconsin noted that while the men were placed in the cornfield, "This was all done under fire of the rebels, so severe that many men were shot down before stepping into line. These shots came over the heads of Jackson's division…neither they nor the enemy could be seen by the twenty-first through the thick corn in front and the woods on the right." Sergeant John Henry Otto of Company D recalled that "[t]he corn was at least 10–12 foot high [so] consequently we were not aware of [Maney's command] coming until they were nearly upon us." Adding to the chaos were the artillery shells that exploded above the drought-stricken stalks, sending shrapnel and wooden sabots into the ranks.[163]

It must have been terrifying for these new soldiers. With some members lying down in the dust and others standing among the dried ears, it was difficult for the new regiment to hold its composure as the sound of gunfire

This image depicts the 21st Wisconsin Infantry crossing the Ohio River into Kentucky from Cincinnati in September 1862. A new regiment, many of the men fell out during the march to Perryville. Many of the neophyte troops had never before fired their rifles. *Courtesy of the Library of Congress.*

Union Colonel Benjamin Sweet commanded the 21st Wisconsin Infantry during the Battle of Perryville. Although he was ill, Sweet moved to the front to lead his regiment. He was severely wounded and taken from the field. *Courtesy of the Library of Congress.*

neared and shrapnel tore through the stalks. Suddenly, "crowds" of Terrill's routed brigade broke through the corn, stomping it down in swaths. The panic quickly caught hold over the new regiment, and several of the 21st Wisconsin fled with their defeated comrades. With no support on their flanks, the lone unit faced Maney's four-regiment front. Fitch wrote that soon "the enemy had lapped both flanks and were in addition to firing in front, enfilading the lines."[164]

A dejected Terrill, miserable after losing the guns on Parsons' ridge, followed his routed brigade through the corn. Fitch recalled that Terrill moved to the rear "almost overcome with vexation and exhaustion." The Unionist Virginian, still clinging to the premise that green troops could rout a superior number of men with the bayonet, told the adjutant of the 21st Wisconsin that the regiment could only survive if it charged the Confederates with bayonets. It was poor advice from a distracted brigade commander, an artillerist by training who, leading infantry for the first time, had just seen his brigade wither away. The adjutant ran for Colonel Sweet, but the ill regimental commander had been wounded and borne from the field.[165]

Fitch wrote that after Terrill departed and the remains of his brigade fled from the corn, "the firing had become terrific, and it seemed at that time strange, that all the firing from the Federal troops, came from the rear of the twenty-first. Reports came from the captains along the line that the men of the twenty-first were being killed by shots from a battery in the rear." Sadly, as the Confederates neared the corn, the Union troops on Starkweather's hill, seventy-five yards behind the 21st Wisconsin, could see the Southerners advancing toward their position. Therefore, these Federals fired at Maney's men, and several of their shots fell short, killing and maiming Wisconsin soldiers in the corn below.[166]

Not only was the 21st Wisconsin subjected to fire from the rear, but the men also endured musketry from Maney's four regiments at their front. When the Confederates neared the corn, the Wisconsinites became caught in a crossfire. Sergeant Otto wrote that "[b]ullets came zipping and whizzing through and over the corn in a lively manner, the first time the men became acquainted with the peculiar hissing 'zipp' a bullet only can make."[167]

For Otto and the other members of the regiment, this baptism of fire was terrifying. Otto wrote:

> *The other Regt. [to the] right and left began a lively fire now; the noise became allmost [sic] deafening. Half a dozen batteries were roaring, shells exploding everywhere; thousands of rifles kept up an incessant rattle. Still*

Above: Placed in a cornfield in front of Starkweather's brigade, the 21st Wisconsin suffered heavily when Maney's Brigade pressed into the stalks. *Courtesy of the Library of Congress.*

Left: Colonel Charles A. McDaniel, commander of the 41st Georgia, sustained a broken hip and a shattered arm while moving through the cornfield toward Starkweather's position. An ordained minister and a former college professor, McDaniel died of his wounds in Harrodsburg, Kentucky, ten days after the fight. *Courtesy of the Perryville Battlefield State Historic Site.*

we did receive no order, or if we did we could not hear it. I got up to get a look around. The 79ᵗʰ [Pennsylvania] and the 24ᵗʰ [Illinois on the hill behind the 21ˢᵗ Wisconsin] were all enveloped in smoke; the first Wis. I could not see on account of the corn. I looked to the front. All at once I saw a rebel flagg [sic], that is, the upper part of it above the cornstalks and not far away neither. I sat down on my right knee and said as loud as I could: "Boys be ready! they ar [sic] coming!"

Otto's comrades immediately knelt down and peered through the corn, dust and smoke. Confusion erupted. Men yelled, "Why don't we fire!" Others looked for their officers, but none could be found. Otto recalled, "I levelled my rifle at some butternut coleured jacked [sic] which I saw among the stalks." The regiment fired. Fitch reported, "Our fighting was done in a corn-field where the rebels did not discover the boys until they rose and discharged the contents of their pieces into them at a distance of twenty yards." Maney's veterans, however, outnumbering the Wisconsin troops by at least three to one, could fire faster and more accurately than these fledgling Federals.[168]

With the Confederates pressing into the stalks and inching closer to the Benton Road, Starkweather's troops vigorously fired into the field. "Right now began our disaster," Otto wrote. "The 1ˢᵗ Wis. on our left and rear had no Rebels on its front, now opened fire towards our front killing and wounding a great number of our own men…I saw som [sic] of our men fall forward and backward." Colonel John Starkweather reported that he had ordered the 21ˢᵗ "to fire and charge the front, but, being a new regiment, their colonel being severely wounded and their major killed about the time such order was given, no field officer was left to carry the command." Several companies fired more than once, but the regiment was forced back, Starkweather wrote, "in some disorder and confusion." The losses were frightful. In addition to Colonel Sweet being gravely wounded, the major, Frederick Shumacher, was killed, shot once in the head and six other times in the chest and legs.[169]

Maney's troops also suffered in the cornfield. Colonel Charles A. McDaniel, the regimental commander of the 41ˢᵗ Georgia, was "severely wounded," sustained a broken hip and was taken from the field. His arm was also shattered and was nearly falling off. An ordained minister and a former college professor, McDaniel died of these injuries in Harrodsburg ten days after the fight. Maney mourned the loss, stating that McDaniel was "an amicable and Christian gentleman [and] a fine discreet and daring officer."[170]

The Confederates overlapped the flanks of the 21st Wisconsin, and the unit fell back. Fitch recalled that the regiment's lone volley momentarily staggered the Southern advance; however, being outnumbered, the troops could not maintain their position. Although the regiment was ordered to retreat, the din of battle made it impossible to hear commands. Therefore, the right side of the 21st wavered and broke. Moments later, the remainder of the unit turned and ran toward Starkweather's position. The bluecoats moving through the corn did not prevent Starkweather's men on the hill from keeping up a steady fire. As the 21st emerged from the stalks and fled across the Benton Road, several men again fell to friendly fire. Starkweather's troops were shooting at anything that moved.[171]

The scattered Federals raced from the corn, with Maney's Brigade tight on their heels. As they reached the road, a "high rail fence" that bordered the lane blocked their path. According to Otto, the fence was a dangerous obstacle. "While running back up the hill and climbing over the fence," he wrote, "the men fell like leaves from a tree in the fall. While trying to mount the fence the strings of both my haversack and canteen were cut in two by a bullet and both fell on the wrong side of the fence. I jumped back to pick them up and just then Sergt. Williams tried to get over the fence. He did not succeed. A bullet hit him in behind in the back passing through the right lung. He fell forward from the fence."[172]

At least one member of Starkweather's 1st Wisconsin admitted that his regiment caused friendly-fire casualties. He noted that "many [members of the regiment] I fear lost their lives in the shower of grape and canister [that was] poured out by the batteries on the rapidly advancing enemy."[173]

Some members of the 21st Wisconsin joined fragments of Terrill's brigade and made a stand at the fence. Major George Kelsoe of the 9th Tennessee reported that when his troops moved across the cornfield toward the Benton Road, "From this fence they poured into our ranks such a destructive fire as to momentarily check our advance, but my men, determined to die rather than to waver, pressed on, in many cases bayoneting the more dogged of our opponents." The three companies of the 105th Ohio that had reformed behind a stone wall that ran along a portion of the road were pushed back by the Confederates when the 1st Tennessee moved forward and formed on the extreme right side of the Rebel line.[174]

The routed members of the 21st Wisconsin crossed the fence, ran across the road and raced up the hill that Starkweather was defending with his infantry and twelve cannons. Michael Fitch of the 21st Wisconsin said that in addition to friendly fire, running up the steep incline of Starkweather's hill was just

Private Christian Weinman of the 21st Wisconsin died from wounds in Springfield, Kentucky, on November 9, one month after the battle. *Courtesy of the Perryville Battlefield State Historic Site.*

as dangerous as climbing the fence. As the ridge was "bare," Fitch recalled, "the fire of the enemy could sweep [it] with terrible effect." When the survivors reached the hilltop, they ran down the backward slope and formed behind the Union line. Some members of the unit, however, remained on top of the ridge. A handful of the soldiers found Starkweather's batteries to be undermanned from artillerists having been killed and wounded, so they helped fire the guns. One, a member of the 21st Wisconsin's Company F named Loewenfeld, had served in the artillery during the German revolution of 1848–49.[175]

The Wisconsinites who passed by the guns and moved "8 or 10 rods behind" Starkweather's hill hastily formed ranks and called roll. When Sergeant Otto formed Company D, he wrote, "I found there were 66 men in line out of 90 with which we had started from Louisville. But where was our Colonel? where [*sic*] was the Major? We learned soon enough. The Colonels [*sic*] left arm was smashed, besides a dangerous wound in the back of the neck, and Major Schumacher was killed. That explained why we did receive no orders while in line, awaiting the rebels."[176]

Of the likely 400 members of the 21st Wisconsin who formed in the cornfield, the regiment lost 39 killed, 103 wounded and 52 missing, for a loss of 49.3 percent of its force. Company F went into the fight with 42 men and lost 12 killed and 16 wounded, with 2 of the wounded dying a few days after the fight. It is known that at least twenty-six members

A modern view, taken from the Benton Road (now Whites Road), looking eastward across the cornfield area toward the back slope of Parsons' Ridge. *Courtesy of the author.*

were captured during the battle. These troops probably fell into Southern hands when the Confederates swept through the cornfield. Some in the regiment believed that they would not have suffered as heavily had they put up greater resistance. Although horribly outnumbered, Otto believed that "[a]lmost every time when a column or Regt. turns to run or retreat from close quarters, the loss on the retreat is more heavy as it would have been had they faced the enemy to the death. So it was with us."[177]

Writing in 1905, Fitch expressed anger over the 21st Wisconsin's placement in the cornfield:

> *The position it was placed in by the commander of the division* [Rousseau], *and left in by the indifference of the brigade commander* [Starkweather], *was the refinement of cruelty. It was between the fire of the enemy and that of our own troops in its immediate rear. The other regiments of the brigade had then been a year in the service and were well drilled and under fine discipline. They were given good positions in rear of the only new regiment*

80

in the brigade. Our correct position was in line with the other regiments on the hill behind. The division commander afterwards denied ordering the regiment to this position, but I know that he did. He gave me the order.[178]

Maney's brigade had taken Parsons' ridge, captured the Union guns and driven off Terrill's infantry. These Tennessee and Georgia soldiers had also swept the novice 21st Wisconsin out of the corn and reached the Benton Road. Their fighting, however, was not over. With Starkweather's infantry and twelve cannons packed on the ridge west of the road, Maney's Brigade would continue to fight for the supremacy of the Federal left flank. Sam Watkins of the 1st Tennessee had anxiously waited for the battle to open. Now he found himself in his most intense fight of the war.

Chapter 9

"MOVE THAT REGIMENT FORWARD"

Maney's Confederates took Parsons' battery, drove off Terrill's brigade, broke the 21st Wisconsin and reached the Benton Road. To continue to crack the Union left flank, Generals Polk and Cheatham ordered Maney to continue his assault against the short but steep ridge that was crammed with Colonel John Starkweather's infantry and twelve cannons. The Federals were fortunate that Starkweather's veteran force had stumbled on this strategically important ridge. According to Starkweather's division commander, Brigadier General Lovell Rousseau, Starkweather "had the good sense when he heard firing in front" to deploy "on the very spot where [his brigade] was most needed."[179]

With the exception of the 21st Wisconsin, Starkweather's brigade was composed of veteran soldiers. On the left (north) side of the hill was Captain Asahel Bush's 4th Battery, Indiana Light Artillery. Organized in Indianapolis on September 15, 1861, Bush's battery was recruited from LaPort, Porter and Lake Counties. These gunners had fought at Shiloh and the siege of Corinth and were armed with two bronze six-pounder Model 1841 rifled James guns, two six-pounder Model 1841 bronze smoothbores and two twelve-pounder bronze smoothbore field howitzers. One member of the battery recalled, "We took position in great haste and under a heavy fire, several horses being shot before we were in position."[180]

On the right (southern) side of the ridge, Starkweather placed Battery A of the 1st Kentucky Artillery. Commanded by Captain David Stone, most of these gunners were from Louisville, with a handful from Indiana and

Captain Asahel Bush commanded the 4th Battery, Indiana Light Artillery. Posted on Starkweather's hill, Bush's battery endured multiple charges from Maney's Brigade, notably the 1st Tennessee Infantry. *Courtesy of the Perryville Battlefield State Historic Site.*

Ohio. Organized in Louisville in September 1861, Stone's battery had also participated in the siege of Corinth. After joining Buell's army at Nashville, members of this battery, with two bronze rifled James guns, two bronze six-pounder Model 1841 smoothbores and two ten-pounder (2.9-inch) Parrott rifles, found themselves fighting for their lives on their native soil.[181]

Supporting these two artillery batteries were Starkweather's veteran infantry regiments. The 1st Wisconsin, commanded by Lieutenant Colonel George B. Bingham, was one of the first regiments that fired into the ranks of the 21st Wisconsin as it fled the cornfield. Organized in Milwaukee in October 1861, the troops wore Federal-issue frock coats with state buttons and forage caps. Men on the line carried .69-caliber rifled muskets, while those on the flank carried .58-caliber rifles. A handful of the soldiers even carried Henry repeating rifles, which had been sold by a vendor on the streets of Louisville before the men marched to Perryville. This fight was likely one of the first battles that this repeater, a precursor to the Winchester lever action, was used in combat.[182]

Starkweather's brigade also included the 24th Illinois Infantry, commanded by Captain August Mauff. Wearing state-issued jackets and armed with .58-caliber rifles on the flank and Belgian muskets in the line, they determined to hold their position at all costs. The brigade also included the 79th Pennsylvania Infantry. Armed with .69-caliber smoothbore muskets and commanded by Colonel Henry Hambright, this regiment was organized in July 1861. It was indeed a local regiment, with nearly all of the soldiers coming from Lancaster County, Pennsylvania. The lone exception was

Union Colonel John Starkweather commanded a brigade of troops from Illinois, Pennsylvania, Wisconsin, Indiana and Kentucky. Starkweather's stand against Maney's Brigade saved the Federal left flank at Perryville. *Courtesy of the Library of Congress.*

Company D, which hailed from Washington County. These Pennsylvanians had served in Missouri, taken a steamer to Cincinnati and then joined Buell's army at Bowling Green. The 79th Pennsylvania found itself in a field immediately south of the hill across the Benton Road.[183]

The brigade's commander was the thirty-two-year-old Colonel John Converse Starkweather, a Cooperstown, New York native who had practiced law in Milwaukee prior to the war. Named colonel of the 1st Wisconsin

Infantry on May 17, 1861, Starkweather led troops in several scrapes before Perryville. Popular in his adopted state of Wisconsin, he was eventually asked to return there to run for governor. Known as an able commander, Colonel John Beatty, who commanded the 3rd Ohio Infantry at Perryville, stated that "Starkweather has the best voice in the army; he can be heard a mile away." Elias Hoover of the 1st Wisconsin recalled that Starkweather "had the boys drilled to precision." This confidence was needed, for his men faced the fight of their lives.[184]

It must have been chilling for Starkweather's command to watch Terrill's brigade crumble against Maney's attack. From their position on the hill three hundred yards west of Parsons' ridge, Starkweather's brigade could see hundreds of blue-coated infantrymen fleeing toward them. Their resolve, however, was bolstered with the arrival of their division commander, Brigadier General Lovell H. Rousseau, who appeared on the hill as Terrill's brigade broke and fled.

Born on August 14, 1818, about twenty miles from Perryville in Lincoln County, Kentucky, Rousseau practiced law in Indiana before joining the state legislature. During the Mexican-American War, Rousseau raised a company of volunteers, became captain and fought at Buena Vista. Upon his return to the Hoosier State, he served in the Indiana legislature and then moved to Louisville, where, in 1860, he was elected to the Kentucky Senate. Although he was initially conciliatory toward the seceding states, when Fort Sumter was bombarded, the proslavery Rousseau hoped that the Federal government would muster the "power to sweep out of existence the miscreants who had done that treason." He opposed Kentucky's initial neutrality and resigned his Senate seat to seek a position in the Union army.

In June 1861, he was commissioned colonel of volunteers. Rousseau immediately went to work recruiting troops. He established Camp Joe Holt across the Ohio River from Louisville, and within three days, he had recruited two infantry regiments and a battery of artillery. Although he was ill at Shiloh, he led a brigade there before fighting around Corinth. According to Union soldier John Fitch, Rousseau helped make "the hills of Chaplin [Perryville] historic." Another Unionist commented that "few men possessed such grand and imposing personal tributes. A finer specimen of manhood has rarely been seen. Add to this, courage, quickness, generosity, and common sense, and you have the basis of heroic character." Of the Federal officers present at Perryville, few performed as ably as Rousseau.[185]

For the Union troops pressed by Maney's Brigade, heroic character was desperately needed. Rousseau rode down Starkweather's line, held his sword

Union Brigadier General Lovell Rousseau, a Kentucky native, commanded a division at Perryville. In several instances, Rousseau rode in front of his troops and twirled his beaver hat on the tip of his sword to rally his men. Of the Union commanders at Perryville, perhaps none performed as ably as Rousseau. *Courtesy of the Library of Congress.*

high above his head and twirled his beaver hat on it. "Now boys," Rousseau shouted above the din, "you stand by me and I will by you and we will whip ---- out of them!" According to a correspondent from the *Louisville Journal*, when Terrill's routed command streamed past Starkweather's position, Rousseau's sword snapped as he tried to beat the panicked troops back into line.[186]

Samuel Starling, adjutant for the slain General Jackson, held a low opinion of his fellow Kentuckian. Starling, who called Rousseau a "large fiery nosed man" and "a demagogue and a sensationalist," wrote that at Perryville Rousseau was "draped in all the finery of war, ostrich feathers, [and] gold lace." Starling noted that Rousseau "dashed down the line in a rapid gallop, with a stern theatrical smile on his face and looked more like the flying Indian in the circus than anything." Despite Starling's criticisms, Rousseau's presence boosted the faltering morale of Starkweather's soldiers.[187]

Many noted Rousseau's calmness under fire. At one point during the battle, some engineers were cowering from the *zip* of bullets. Rousseau simply told them, "Oh, never mind those little things!" The group was immediately spotted by Confederate artillerymen, who launched a shell over their heads. Rousseau instinctively ducked and added, "but d--n the big ones."[188]

Although his sword broke while rallying his soldiers, Rousseau's efforts were successful. Captain Robert Taylor, who was driven off Parsons' ridge by Maney's command with the rest of Garrard's detachment, found Rousseau's display to be emboldening. Taylor remarked, "[O]ur Division had suffered defeat after defeat, until I began to fear the day had gone against us; but when I saw Rousseau's men climbing up the hill with the steady step of veterans…and saw their stalwart leader raising his cap to the front of his sword [and] elevate his arm to its utmost stretch, and whirl it high in the air over his head. I knew it meant victory, and I almost wept with joy."[189]

After taking Parsons' ridge, Maney's Brigade moved through a short belt of woods before forcing the 21st Wisconsin from the cornfield. There, part of Confederate Brigadier General A.P. Stewart's brigade joined Maney's command. Stewart's 5th Tennessee Infantry Regiment formed next to the 9th Tennessee on Maney's extreme left, providing the Confederates with a five-regiment front as they moved against Starkweather's position. The exhausted troops advanced across the Benton Road and assaulted the hill but were repulsed. According to Colonel George C. Porter of the 6th Tennessee, the men re-formed in a ravine near the fence along the Benton Road before Maney again ordered them to attack. When Confederate officers feared that Union troops could outflank them, Cheatham ordered the 1st Tennessee, which was still behind Maney's other regiments, to move to the extreme right to deploy on the northernmost point of the battlefield. The division commander later explained, "I gave General Maney orders to move that regiment forward and capture those guns." Because Maney's first line was exhausted, the burden of capturing Starkweather's hill fell mostly on the 1st Tennessee for the remainder of the day.[190]

A modern view looking west from Parsons' ridge toward Starkweather's hill. At the time of the battle, a cornfield grew in the ravine between the two ridges. Benton Road (now Whites Road) is located at the base of Starkweather's hill, where a portion of Union Colonel John C. Starkweather's brigade and twelve cannons were positioned. *Courtesy of the author.*

Colonel Hume Feild, the commander of the 1st Tennessee who had led the other four regiments during Maney's absence, received Cheatham's directive to take the hill. According to Feild, Starkweather's artillery was ripping apart the right wing of the brigade. Therefore, he asked Maney if the 1st Tennessee could move to the right to support this flank. The 1st tromped northward through the body-strewn cornfield. Upon reaching the base of Starkweather's hill, Feild turned and faced his men, drew his sword and shouted, "Follow me!" With a yell, the 1st Tennessee charged up the slope.[191]

According to Maney, "The 1st Tenn. Regt. went forward most gallantly and in perfect order." Feild noted that the attack was undertaken "in splendid style, with close, compact ranks, killing all the horses and men of the battery and driving its support away." A Hoosier artilleryman commented that the Rebels "made a desperate charge to turn our left. They advanced through a cornfield and up the hill in the face of the fire of our two Batteries." The Confederates were driven back, and the 1st Tennessee lost more than forty men killed in this first charge.[192]

As the 1st Tennessee attacked the northern side of the slope, the remnants of Maney's other regiments assaulted other portions of the hill. The 27th Tennessee fought across the Benton Road twice but was forced back, Colonel Frierson wrote, when the regiment "met with stout resistance." Major George Kelsoe of the 9th Tennessee remarked that the brigade was hit hard. The men were raked with "musketry fire in our front and the grape and canister shots that fell like hail from a third battery to our right…a most murderous fire was poured into our flank from a thicket on our left." Although this flanking fire from the 79th Pennsylvania was dangerous, Kelsoe noted that the artillery fire was most damaging. Stone and Bush's batteries emitted "a fire of grape and canister which our oldest veterans had never seen equaled, [but the regiment] pressed on all unmindful of the carnage surrounding them." As soon as the charge began across the Benton Road, Kelsoe's horse was shot out from under him.[193]

Sergeant Edward Ferguson of the 1st Wisconsin, who was wounded twice at Perryville, noted the severity of the defense. "The dense cloud of smoke from the rapid discharge of cannon and advancing musketry hid the enemy with an almost impenetrable veil," Ferguson wrote. A *Louisville Journal* correspondent agreed. He reported that "Stone's men shouted and laughed like devils at every shot. The gunners caught the pieces ere their recoil had been completed and pushed them into position. The rapid firing of musketry and artillery here was never before excelled, and a perfect hailstorm of shell and solid shot fell among them." The correspondent added, "It was a glorious sight worth the danger and exposure to witness." The next day, Federal officers toured this portion of the battlefield and recorded the gruesome effect that these guns had on Maney's Brigade.[194]

Some of the Union artillerymen were members of the routed 21st Wisconsin, and they took to the guns when they realized that the pieces were undermanned. As these novice infantrymen blasted canister at the gray ranks, Starkweather approached the artillery and asked, "Who runs this cannon?" Sergeant John Otto replied, "Colonel, we are running this business on shares, but Loewenfeld [who served in the German Revolution] serves as a Captain without a commission." Above the noise, Starkweather shouted, "Well, give them hell!" and moved off to the left.[195]

The Federals kept up an obstinate defense against Maney's onslaught, but casualties mounted. Captain William Mitchell of the 1st Wisconsin explained the attack in a letter to his father. "We were supporting a Battery, [with] the 21st Wis in front of us when a whole Rebel Brigade charged our Battery. The 21st broke and ran over us in the rear…My boys fought like tigers."[196]

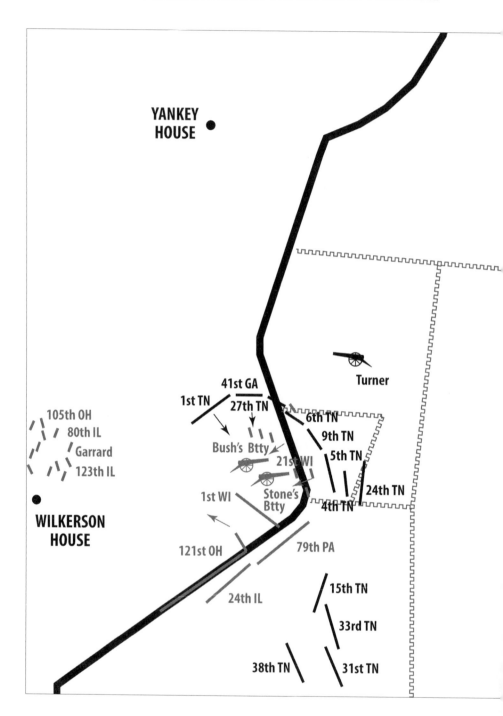

3:30 p.m.

**WALKER
HOUSE**
●

**KIRKLAND
HOUSE**
●

This map, based on maps created by Perryville park manager Kurt Holman, shows Maney's Brigade attacking Starkweather's hill while Brigadier General A.P. Stewart advances alongside of Maney's command. This map depicts the action on the extreme Union left flank at about 3:30 p.m. *Map design courtesy of Charley Pallos.*

Private Sam Watkins of the 1ˢᵗ Tennessee vividly described the assault in his postwar memoir, *Co. Aytch*. As his regiment moved toward Bush's battery on the north side of Starkweather's line, Watkins wrote:

> *We did not recoil, but our line was fairly hurled back by the leaden hail that was poured into our very faces. Eight color-bearers were killed at one discharge of their cannon…It was death to retreat now to either side. Our Lieutenant-Colonel Patterson halloed to charge and take their guns, and we were soon in a hand-to-hand fight—every man for himself—using the butts of our guns and bayonets…Such obstinate fighting I never had seen before or since. The guns were discharged so rapidly that it seemed the earth itself was in a volcanic uproar. The iron storm passed through our ranks, mangling and tearing men to pieces. The very air seemed full of stifling smoke and fire which seemed the very pit of hell, peopled by contending demons.* [197]

The 1ˢᵗ Tennessee suffered heavily during the first charge up the hill. While Watkins was lucky to emerge from the battle unscathed (though he "was shot through the hat and cartridge box"), John A. Bruce of Company B was not so fortunate. Like Watkins, Bruce recalled that a shower of lead rained on them. Bruce wrote his brother that "I was not in the fight very long, only fired five rounds before I was shot down. We had nearly reached a battery we were charging at the time. One ball struck my clothes lightly, one went through my coat sleeve, one through my coat pocket, one took off my cartridge box, one went through my haversack, and the next one brought me down while in the act of loading."

Struck in the thigh, Bruce walked sixty feet before collapsing. He lay in the dried grass, watched the fight unfold and soon saw Lieutenant Colonel John Patterson fall from his horse. Moments later, a member of the 1ˢᵗ Tennessee led Patterson's horse over to Bruce, put the wounded soldier on it and led Bruce to the rear. Bruce later informed his sibling, "I have the bullet which struck me. It struck something beforehand, as it was split in two." After the fight, Bruce was captured by the Federals when his field hospital fell into Union hands. Taken to a hospital about twenty miles away in Lebanon, he was eventually sent to prison at Camp Chase, Ohio, where he remained for one year until he was exchanged. Bruce's luck did not hold. Although he survived six bullets on Starkweather's hill, he died in a train wreck near Liberty, Virginia, in April 1863. [198]

Like the wounded Bruce, many members of the 1ˢᵗ Tennessee witnessed the conspicuous death of their beloved lieutenant colonel, John Patterson, a

Private Sam Watkins of the 1st Tennessee Infantry attacked Starkweather's hill along with the rest of Maney's Brigade. After the battle, Watkins removed several seriously wounded comrades from the battlefield. *Courtesy of the Perryville Battlefield State Historic Site.*

leader whom Maney called "a most estimable gentleman and excellent officer." Marcus Toney of Company B reported that shortly after the charge commenced, "Colonel Patterson was slightly wounded in the wrist, but he tied a handkerchief around it and continued to give orders until a grapeshot hit his moustache, going through his head, killing him instantly." Watkins recalled that Patterson "was killed standing right by my side. He was first shot through the hand, and was wrapping his handkerchief around it, when another ball struck and killed him."[199]

One particularly youthful member of the 1st Tennessee nearly died while charging the Union position. Watkins "saw W.J. Whittorne, then a strippling boy of fifteen years of age, fall, shot through the neck and collarbone. He fell apparently dead, when I saw him all at once jump up, grab his gun and commence loading and firing, and I heard him say, 'D--n 'em, I'll fight 'em as long as I live.'" The young soldier survived the battle and the war.[200]

Since two brigades were fighting for control of such a narrow hill, the number of bullets fired in such a small space created heavy casualties. Four days after the fight, Captain William Mitchell of the 1st Wisconsin lamented that "Poor Billy Brown died at my side as Brave and good a boy as ever shouldered a musket. He was shot through the right breast, the Ball taking an angling course, and I think touched the Heart. He fell and as he did I grasped his hand & heard his last & only words 'Capt My God.'" Mitchell added that another one of his men "thinks he was shot by some of our men as the Ball entered his thigh from behind." This was possible, given the friendly-fire experiences of the 21st Wisconsin, but it is also possible the soldier caught the bullet while running from the fight. Confederate artillery also came into play against the 1st Wisconsin. The regimental banner was struck by a solid shot.[201]

The Wisconsin regiments and the 1st Tennessee were not the only units to suffer during Maney's initial assault against Starkweather's line. When the 9th Tennessee joined the attack, every company commander was either killed or wounded. Furthermore, among the dead were William Rhodes and Frank Buck of the 27th Tennessee, the two ashen-faced lads who had informed their captain that they would be killed in the day's fight. Despite the casualties, Maney's men made it to the top of the hill, where a hand-to-hand fight erupted around the wheels of the guns. One of Bush's artillerymen recalled, "Their line of bayonets were within a few feet of our guns"; for an instant, the flag of the 1st Tennessee was shot down and fell between the artillery pieces.[202]

According to Maney, "after a short but severe and bloody" contest, his brigade took the hill. The men, however, rapidly began to fall back. Soldiers in the 1st Tennessee told Thomas Malone, Maney's adjutant, that Lieutenant Colonel Patterson had ordered the retreat. Patterson, however, had been killed. When Patterson's horse moved to the rear with the wounded John Bruce, several soldiers believed that a general retreat had been ordered. The brigade moved down the hill and took cover next to the Benton Road. Colonel Feild, realizing that the 1st Tennessee had nearly captured the ridge before the accidental withdrawal, ordered the troops to attack the slope a second time. The Union gunners, who had been driven away from the cannons by the fierce hand-to-hand struggle, returned to their pieces when Feild reformed his lines at the base of the hill.[203]

Sergeant Otto of the 21st Wisconsin, helping fire the Union cannons, was caught in the Confederate advance and rapid withdrawal. Otto remarked that his battery had just loaded the guns with double canister when

> *the rebels were just tearing down the fence intending to capture the battery. They got the compliment* [sic] *from the battery right among them. Just then the 79th [Pennsylvania] and 1st Wis. Poured a terrible flank fire from both flanks into their ranks. They staggered for a moment then turned back on the retreat* [just] *when we had the second charge ready, which they received as a farewell. When they got out of reach of canister we loaded shells and hurled the same after them as an acknowledgment of their friendly visit.[204]*

94

During the first charge up Starkweather's hill, other nearby Confederate units tried to aid the assault. When the 1st Tennessee moved forward, Colonel John Wharton's cavalry—consisting of Kentucky, Tennessee, Texas and Georgia horsemen—was ordered to strike Starkweather's line on the extreme left flank. The troopers moved from Wilson's Creek, located north of Starkweather's position, and rode southward while Maney's regiments assaulted the hill from the east. When Wharton's men charged, Bush's artillery battery poured an intense fire into their ranks. One member of the 8th Texas Cavalry remarked, "Under this fire of artillery we had a complete set of fours cut down by one cannon ball or shell that passed through the bodies of four horses, cutting off both legs of one man below the knee but not injuring the other three men, who mounted behind other comrades and rode off the field." Among the casualties was Captain Mark Evans, commander of the 8th Texas Cavalry (Terry's Texas Rangers). Because of the accuracy of the Union guns, Wharton canceled the charge, noting that "it was useless to have men and horses killed in charging a half mile in an open field."[205]

Maney's Rebels were also joined by part of Stewart's Brigade, which, after receiving no orders, had initially remained in position behind the ridge near the Chaplin River. Upon learning that Donelson's Brigade needed support, Stewart advanced his five regiments—the 4th, 5th, 24th, 33rd and 31st Tennessee Infantry Regiments—in one long line. As Maney's men neared the Benton Road after the collapse of Terrill's second position between the cornfield and Parsons' ridge, Stewart's 5th Tennessee appeared on Maney's left, while the 4th Tennessee, in reserve, supported its attack. This aided the overall Confederate advance, for a gap existed between Donelson's Brigade, which had opened the battle, and Maney's command. Stewart's Brigade plugged this gap and assisted in pushing back the Union troops south of Maney's position.[206]

Born in Rogersville, Tennessee, on October 21, 1821, Stewart was an 1841 graduate of the United States Military Academy. Upon his graduation from West Point, Stewart served one year in the 3rd U.S. Artillery before returning to the academy to teach mathematics. Although he resigned after two years because of ill health, Stewart continued teaching at Cumberland University in Lebanon, Tennessee, and at the University of Nashville. When the Civil War erupted, Stewart was a mathematics professor at Cumberland University. Because of his military education and experience, he was commissioned major of artillery in the Provisional Army of Tennessee. When these state troops joined Confederate service, Stewart was named brigadier

A modern view taken from Starkweather's hill, looking eastward over the Benton Road (now Whites Road) and across the cornfield. The back slope of Parsons' ridge is in the distance. *Courtesy of the author.*

general and soon saw combat. In November 1861, he fought at Belmont and later led troops at Shiloh. James D. Porter, who became adjutant general of Cheatham's Division, called Stewart "a fine specimen of a man. Tennessee never produced a better soldier or a more perfect gentleman."[207]

As Stewart's 5th Tennessee pressed westward on Maney's left, it was shelled by Captain David Stone's Kentucky battery and was fired on by Starkweather's 79th Pennsylvania, which commanded a field immediately south of Starkweather's ridge. Stewart's men emerged from some woods, but the rapidity with which the Pennsylvanians could fire their muskets sent panic through the ranks. At one point, many of Stewart's men were killed while trying to crowd through an opening in a rail fence rather than climbing over it. Cooler heads prevailed, however, and the regiment pressed forward against Starkweather's line.[208]

Like the other regiments in that sector of the battlefield, casualties were heavy. During one charge, a soldier named Rucker in Stewart's 4th Tennessee was shot in the forehead. The ball peeled up a portion of the man's scalp.

Confederate Brigadier General Alexander P. Stewart commanded a brigade in Cheatham's Division. Stewart's troops attacked shortly after Maney's command deployed and filled a gap that had opened between Donelson's Brigade and Maney's soldiers. *Courtesy of the Library of Congress.*

The soldier threw down his weapon and exclaimed, "There! That would have killed brother George as dead as Hector!" George was an inch taller than Rucker, who was an amazing six feet, six inches tall. Had Rucker been any taller, the bullet would have struck him in the brain instead of parting his hair in this most uncomfortable fashion.[209]

When the 5th Tennessee supported Maney's attack on Starkweather's hill, Benjamin A. Hagnewood of Company A was struck in the chest by a ramrod that had been left in the muzzle of a Pennsylvanian's gun. Hagnewood fell unconscious and awoke to discover, he wrote, "the butt end of a steel rammer sticking out of my left breast." The soldier eventually pulled the ramrod out of his chest and made his way to a field hospital. Perryville was the 79th Pennsylvania's first battle, and several of the green troops forgot to remove their ramrods before firing. Because Stewart's men were using "buck and ball" rounds, which consisted of a musket ball and three buckshot, wounds were also prevalent on the Federal side. Pennsylvanian William Clark was wounded three times but continued to fight. He suffered a flesh wound in the side and caught buckshot

Private Emanuel Rudy of the 79th Pennsylvania was wounded at Perryville and died from his injury on October 12, three days after the fight. *Courtesy of the Perryville Battlefield State Historic Site.*

in the elbow and shoulder. His fellow soldier William Woodward was also injured by a "buck and ball" round. Woodward endured a serious lung wound and lost part of his ear and a piece of his finger. A Union soldier who battled against Stewart's men near the Benton Road noted that the "ground was covered with [the] blood" of the Federal casualties.[210]

With the assistance of the 24th Tennessee, the 5th Tennessee pushed the 79th Pennsylvania from its position. Although the 24th Tennessee eventually fell back from exhaustion, the 5th Tennessee continued to press its advantage. Its hopes of fully routing the Pennsylvanians were stifled, however, when Stone's battery blasted the troops with canister. The men rallied and continued forward, but the survivors of the 79th Pennsylvania checked the Tennesseans' advance. Soon enough, Maney's Brigade would wish that Stewart's regiments had sustained their momentum. The Federals' ability to stem the tide of Stewart's assault would have dire consequences for the 1st Tennessee.[211]

Chapter 10

"UNABATED FURY"

Maney's Brigade was exhausted. The 1st Tennessee, spearheading the attack against Starkweather's line, had struggled in a hand-to-hand contest against the enemy and had lost more than forty killed and dozens wounded. Maney's four other regiments were also spent. These men had fought for every inch of soil on that hot, dry October day, and their commanders could not force them forward another foot. With the exception of the 1st Tennessee, most of Maney's men were spent and were unable to continue the attack.

As the 1st Tennessee rallied near the northern base of the hill, its brigade commander approached. Maney had led these men in western Virginia and at Shiloh. He had depended on their fighting spirit before, and Perryville was no different. With Stewart pressing the enemy to their left, Maney urged the men to attack. Colonel Feild barked his orders, and the 1st Tennessee, along with a handful of men from the other regiments, somehow rose to their feet and again attacked. Maney then moved off to the left to re-form his battered regiments that waited near the Benton Road.[212]

The renewed assault was aided by crucial artillery support. As the men prepared to attack, Captain William Carnes's Tennessee artillery battery, attached to Donelson's Brigade, moved to the northeast and fired on Starkweather's line, enfilading the Union left flank. Furthermore, Turner's Battery moved forward and dropped shells on Starkweather's center from Parsons' ridge. Turner's men fired until Cheatham ordered the battery to cease fire and move to the rear so that the Confederate infantry could resume their assault.[213]

Carnes played a pivotal role in aiding the 1st Tennessee. His coolness in directing guns had been forged during a unique military career. Born in Memphis in 1840, Carnes was the son of a prominent planter. A graduate of the U.S. Naval Academy, after the outbreak of national hostilities Carnes was named drillmaster of the 5th Tennessee Infantry. This role proved to be brief, however, for he quickly joined the artillery. At age twenty, Carnes was named captain, a promotion that made him the youngest artillery captain in the Confederacy at that time. His peers recognized his gift for commanding heavy guns. In late 1863, Confederate Brigadier General Marcus J. Wright informed Carnes that no soldier under Southern arms "has been more conspicuous for gallantry in action and general worth or as an officer…in all that makes up the brave, intelligent, and reliable officer I know no one in the Army that surpasses you."[214]

Captain Thomas J. Stanford and his Mississippi artillery battery joined Carnes on the far right. According to Stanford, he had been ordered to move "onward in the direction of the heaviest firing," so he led his command to the extreme northern flank of the Southern line. In addition to fighting at Shiloh and Perryville, Stanford's battery eventually fought at Murfreesboro, Chickamauga, Missionary Ridge and in the Atlanta Campaign. These men were renowned for their bravery. During one battle, gunner J.S. McMath "was the last man to leave his gun, and he was then covered with blood of the many comrades who had been shot down near him. Few would have remained there so long."[215]

With the Rebel artillery pounding the hill, Maney's Brigade surged forward. The 1st Tennessee moved up on the right, while fragments of the 9th Tennessee and 6th Tennessee mustered the strength to advance on the left. The 27th Tennessee and the 41st Georgia were so decimated that few of their soldiers attacked. Facing the 1st Wisconsin, parts of the 121st Ohio, 21st Wisconsin, Garrard's detachment and a smattering of troops from Terrill's vanquished brigade, the 1st Tennessee again battled the 1st Wisconsin. Stewart's 5th Tennessee continued to press the 79th Pennsylvania.[216]

During this assault, Malone had his personal belief "that a man cannot escape his fate" confirmed. While lambasting a soldier who was hiding in a three-foot ditch, Malone contended, "a ball, coming from the Lord knows where, struck him and killed him while I was talking to him."[217]

While this unfortunate soldier was hiding from the horrors of Starkweather's hill, the rest of Maney's command was advancing, enduring the shell and musketry. According to Maney, patriotic motives inspired the men. "Advancing again to the hill top," he recalled, "the 1st [Tennessee] resumed the attack upon immensely superior numbers there fighting with the desperation inspired by the memory of invaded and outraged homes[.] [N]umbers could not resist its valor and deadly vollies [*sic*] and the enemy in front was broken and driven before them."[218]

According to Captain Robert Taylor of Garrard's detachment, the horrors of the fight washed patriotic motives from his comrades' hearts. As he moved forward to support Bush's battery, he found that "the ground around was slippery with blood, many a poor dark looking powder begrimed Artillery man was laying stretched out upon the ground around us, torn and mutilated, their countenance plainly indicating the awful manner of their death."[219]

While some troops cowered from the gunfire and artillery, acts of heroism inspired soldiers on both sides. As the 1st Tennessee slammed into the ranks of the 1st Wisconsin, Sergeant John Durham of Company F, 1st Wisconsin, grabbed his regimental flag when the color sergeant was hit. Durham then ran between the opposing lines and waved the flag "amid a shower of shot, shell, and bullets," until his commanding officer stopped him. On November 20, 1896, Durham was awarded the Medal of Honor for his help in rallying Starkweather's tired brigade.[220]

While the fighting raged on Starkweather's hill, Terrill's brigade regrouped about 250 yards behind (west) of Starkweather's position. Terrill saw his shattered command re-form, his depression lifted and he again became interested in the struggle. After ordering his command forward to support Bush's battery, the Unionist Virginian moved to the front.[221]

Terrill's story, which showcases the fratricidal nature of the conflict, is one of the most intriguing to emerge from the Civil War. Born in Covington, Virginia, on April 21, 1834, Terrill was the son of a prominent lawyer and congressman who was related to both J.E.B. Stuart and Robert E. Lee. Terrill graduated sixteenth in his West Point class of 1853. His tenacity was evident as a student; he once came to blows with fellow cadet Philip Sheridan after Sheridan attacked him with a bayonet. Upon graduation, Terrill was assigned to the U.S. Artillery, where he fought in the Seminole War. Like his counterpart A.P. Stewart, Terrill returned to the U.S. Military Academy to teach mathematics. With the advent of the Civil War, Terrill, despite his Virginia birth, remained in the Federal army. When offered a post in the Confederate service, Terrill responded, "The Union cause, to which I have devoted my life, has nothing but honor to endear it, and it has no terror but that of death, which a soldier must always expect. The rebellion however offers nothing but dishonor and disgrace, and I shall adhere to the flag of the Union and give my life if necessary in support of the legally constituted government of the United States." He was one of sixteen Virginians who held prewar commissions who fought for the North. The remaining forty-seven joined the Confederacy. When he embraced Unionism, Terrill's family was crushed. His dismayed father wrote him, "Can you be so recreant and so unnatural as to aid in the mad attempt to impose the yoke of tyranny upon your kith and kin? Do so and your name shall be stricken from the family records."[222]

Despite the threat from his father, William remained loyal to the Union while his brother, James, joined the Confederacy. An 1858 graduate of the Virginia Military Institute, James served in the 13th Virginia Infantry. In May 1861, Unionist brother William was appointed captain of the 5th U.S. Artillery. Soon, the officer was named chief of artillery for the 2nd Division of the Army of the Ohio; he won praise for his performance at the Battle of Shiloh and was promoted to brigadier general. The Battle of Perryville was his first brigade command.[223]

Some of Terrill's troops—especially members of the 105th Ohio—despised their brigade commander. According to Buckeye Stanley Lockwood, Terrill once knocked a man over the head with his sword for leaving the ranks on a hot day. Lockwood referred to Terrill as "a drunken old tyrant and deserves to be shot by his own men and if he don't come to that fate it will be because the oath of hundreds of men in the 105th Regiment is good for nothing." Others, namely officers, disagreed with this assessment. Captain Samuel Starling referred to Terrill as "a first rate fighting man," while another Federal officer called Terrill "an earnest, faithful soldier and Christian gentleman." No matter what these soldiers thought of Terrill, Confederate artillerymen at Perryville would carry out the oaths of the disgruntled members of the 105th Ohio.[224]

Near 4:00 p.m., as Terrill followed his reorganized brigade up the back slope of Starkweather's hill, a Confederate artillery shell (likely fired from Captain William Carnes's battery) exploded above the Union general. Shrapnel tore through the left side of Terrill's chest, carrying away part of his lung. Major James A. Connolly of the 123rd Illinois was within five feet of Terrill when the shell exploded. "I was the only one with him," Connolly wrote. "I raised him to a sitting position, and saw that nearly his entire breast was torn away by the shell. He recognized me and his first words were: 'Major, do you think it is fatal?' I knew it must be, but to encourage him I answered, 'Oh I hope not General.' He then said: 'My poor wife, my poor wife.'" Taken to the Wilkerson House, located about two hundred yards to the northwest, the Unionist Virginian died at about 2:00 a.m. the next morning. Command of the 33rd Brigade passed to Colonel Albert Hall, leader of the 105th Ohio Infantry.[225]

Union Brigadier General William R. Terrill commanded the 33rd Brigade at Perryville. His brigade was shoved away from Parsons' ridge by Maney's troops. Terrill was later mortally wounded by an artillery shell fragment when he returned to the action. *Courtesy of the Kentucky Historical Society.*

Terrill's father, who swore that his elder son would be disinherited, surely regretted the loss of his son. His grief was horribly compounded when Terrill's younger Confederate brother, James, was killed at Bethesda Church, Virginia, during the Cold Harbor Campaign. In an act of guilt-ridden contrition, their father reputedly placed a memorial stone in honor of his children that read, "This monument erected by their father. God alone knows which was right."[226]

Shortly after Terrill was mortally wounded, the Union lines on Starkweather's hill crumbled. The shattered Federal force, beaten back by Maney's exhausted brigade, began a hasty westward withdrawal. While the 79th Pennsylvania, 24th Illinois and 1st Wisconsin held the line, Starkweather ordered the artillery pulled back. Since so many of the artillerymen and horses had been killed (at least thirty-five horses died on the ridge), the Union soldiers feared that the two batteries would fall into enemy hands. To save the guns, several companies of the 1st Wisconsin dragged the cannons off by hand. As the bluecoats strained to remove the artillery, Private William Wechselberg of Company D, 1st Wisconsin, was shot in the head and killed. In addition to the Southern gunfire, Carnes's Battery shelled the retreating Union soldiers. Only two of Bush's four guns were saved. William M. Pollard of the 1st Tennessee recorded in his diary, "We charged and captured several pieces of artillery at a terrible loss." He added that Company B of the 1st

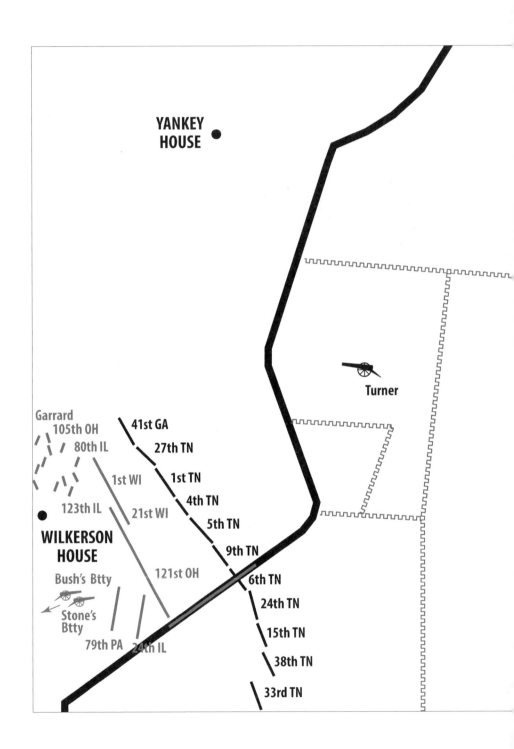

4:00 p.m.

**WALKER
HOUSE**
●

**KIRKLAND
HOUSE**
●

This map, based on maps created by Perryville park manager Kurt Holman, shows Maney's Brigade continuing its attack against Starkweather's men after these Union troops fell back to a ridge immediately west of their initial position. This map depicts the action on the extreme Union left flank at about 4:00 p.m. Starkweather's men held this position and saved the Federal left flank. *Map design courtesy of Charley Pallos.*

Tennessee lost twenty out of twenty-six men, including "every commissioned and non-commissioned officer except the fourth corporal, a boy 19 years of age, who came out in command of the company."[227]

The Union soldiers withdrew to another ridge one hundred yards west of Starkweather's initial line. The rolling terrain around Perryville enabled the Federals to establish successive defensive positions on consecutive hilltops. This fighting from one ridge to another helped exhaust Maney's regiments and ultimately ensured the safety of the Union left flank.

After taking Starkweather's hill, Maney's 6th and 9th Tennessee, aided by Stewart's 4th Tennessee, moved forward to attack the Federals' new position. These regiments moved against the left side of the hill. Some of Bush and Stone's cannons were positioned on the ridge, and here the Union troops rallied. As Maney's command attacked, the surviving artillerymen, portions of Terrill's brigade, the 121st Ohio, 79th Pennsylvania, 24th Illinois and the 1st Wisconsin formed on the corn-covered ridge.[228]

When the Confederates struck this new position, the 9th Tennessee got within fifty yards of Stone's guns. Stewart recalled that his men pushed the enemy back until they reached "the crest of a ridge which terminated on the right in a cornfield." There the regiments halted. Although they momentarily exchanged volleys with the reassembled Union line, the troops, Stewart remarked, "were compelled to halt & fall back to the front of the ridge for want of ammunition." Unable to secure rifle cartridges, Stewart withdrew his men eastward, where they halted about one hundred yards from the Federal position. Other members of Maney's Brigade, also fighting to the left of the 1st Tennessee, fell back. This withdrawal proved to be costly for the 1st Tennessee.[229]

The 1st Tennessee continued to battle on the extreme right of the Rebel line as Stewart and Maney's other regiments pushed the Union troops back. As most of Starkweather's command deployed on the corn-covered ridge, the 1st Wisconsin and a handful of other troops formed behind a limestone wall that ran along the northern end of the hill. The 1st Tennessee moved forward against the Union soldiers behind the wall. According to John Magee of Stanford's Battery, "The enemy were behind a stone fence firing at our men. We threw a few hundred shells into them, which soon made them leave, and our men charged them." Magee added, "The battle now raged with unabated fury all along the line—the roar of musketry was terrific while the booming of cannon was unceasing."[230]

Colonel Albert Hall of the 105th Ohio, now commanding Terrill's brigade, joined Starkweather's new line. Hall reported:

The fire at this moment was terrific beyond description, and the running through my line of a six-horse team drawing a caisson created some disorder in my center. At almost the same moment of this repulse of the enemy [Stewart's brigade] *a determined assault was made by them* [the 1st Tennessee] *on our left. A battery opened on us from the enemy's right* [Carnes's Battery], *and from the form of the ground nearly enfiladed my line.*[231]

Private Sam Watkins found humor in one surreal moment while the 1st Tennessee attacked. "I remember one little incident that I laughed at while in the very midst of battle," Watkins recalled. "We were charging through an old citizen's yard, when a big yellow cur dog ran out and commenced snapping at the soldiers' legs—they kicking at him to keep him off. The next morning he was lying near the same place, but he was a dead dog."[232]

Another member of the 1st Tennessee, Lieutenant Charles King of Company I, was celebrating his twenty-seventh birthday during the Battle of Perryville. Born on October 8, 1835, King had enlisted as a lieutenant in the regiment in April 1861. Immediately before the Perryville Campaign, King had been offered the colonelcy in another unit but had declined in order to remain with the 1st Tennessee. At Perryville, King was conspicuous in leading his men and was wounded in his left forearm. He probably never envisioned that he would spend a birthday in the midst of such carnage.[233]

When Stewart's men ran out of ammunition and withdrew, the left flank of Feild's 1st Tennessee was left "hanging in the air," vulnerable to Federal enfilade fire. As Stewart pulled back, two Union regiments moved forward and blasted the left flank of the 1st Tennessee. Maney noted that his Tennesseans' success "was checked by a heavy and deadly flank fire from the left" and that "our line to the left was not advanced sufficiently to protect the flank in that direction."[234]

Although the assault against the 1st Wisconsin was stifled, Feild was determined to hold the line. As Feild looked southward, he wrote, "I discovered Hardee's battle-flag coming up on our left." Thinking that these Confederates would attack the two Yankee regiments that were enfilading his line, Feild "determined to hold the hill at every cost." Much to Feild's disappointment, these Confederate regiments withdrew, and the Tennesseans fell back toward Starkweather's first location. Private Marcus Toney of the 1st Tennessee simply noted that the regiment was "subjected to an enfilade fire from the enemy, which played havoc with our men."[235]

According to Maney, Feild had no choice but to withdraw. With Stewart forced back, the fire from the left "raked" the 1st Tennessee with a renewed

The Battle of Perryville, as depicted by artist Henry Moesler. *Courtesy of the Kentucky Historical Society.*

intensity. In addition, the Wisconsin troops behind the stone wall—including a handful of men armed with Henry repeaters—re-formed and fired on Feild's front. With attacks coming from the south and the west, Maney wrote, "it was sheer madness to attempt to advance further or hold longer the exposed position and the Regt. after perhaps one of the bloodiest and fiercest contests of the war for the numbers engaged was compelled to fall back."[236]

Another surprising event also forced the tired Tennesseans to withdraw. Although casualties were severe in the Wisconsin regiments, portions of the 1st and 21st Wisconsin regiments caught their breath and counterattacked. The Union troops, according to Starkweather, "charged to the front," and Private Morris Rice of Company H, 1st Wisconsin, captured the battle flag of either the 27th or the 1st Tennessee.[237]

Feild was depressed from the losses that were sustained when Stewart's command and Maney's other regiments fell back on his left. He explained in his diary that "seeing that to hold their ground meant the destruction of the whole command, I withdrew the regiment after sacrificing the best and noblest blood of Tennessee to a mistaken order. Twenty-three or four commissioned officers were killed and wounded in the two assaults." He also reported that he left "half" of the regiment "dead and wounded on the top of the hill."[238]

As Maney's command fell back toward Parsons' ridge, Terrill's brigade and Starkweather's regiments withdrew to the west. These Union troops halted several hundred yards behind the stone wall and north of the Dixville Crossroads, the intersection where the Mackville Road met the Benton Road. At the end of the battle, after both Union flanks had been shoved back toward the crossroads, the Union troops spent the remainder of the night moving their supplies and equipment onto the Dixville Road, toward the rest of their army. Once their lines of communication were secured, the Federals abandoned the intersection and pulled back to a new defensive position, a chain of hills located a few hundred yards northwest of the crossroads. Night was falling, and Sergeant Otto of the 21st Wisconsin was relieved that his first battle was over. He was, he wrote, "thankfull [sic] to Miss Luna for showing us her bright, if cold face, turning night into day. By her bright light we were enabled to look after, and gather the numerous wounded who lay plentyfully [sic] scattered all over the field."[239]

The stand made by Starkweather's brigade was a critical phase in the Battle of Perryville. Starkweather's stubborn defense of the Union left, coupled with the Confederates' inability to seize the Dixville Crossroads, saved McCook's corps. Had Starkweather's brigade been destroyed, the intersection would have been left wide open for the Confederates, who could have slipped behind McCook's right wing, thereby cutting him off from the rest of Buell's army. Had the crossroads been seized, McCook's corps could have been annihilated.

The Union troops on the northern end of the battlefield suffered for their success. Starkweather stated, "My loss in officers and men was terrible indeed." Of Starkweather's 2,514 men, 169 were killed, 476 were wounded and 103 were missing. These 748 casualties constituted a loss of 30 percent of his force.[240]

The 21st Wisconsin, fighting alone and unsupported in the cornfield, lost 39 killed, 103 wounded and 52 missing. Also among the losses were Starkweather's artillerymen, whose blood literally covered the ground among the guns. Captain David Stone's Kentucky battery lost 3 killed, 10 wounded and 1 missing, while Captain Asahel Bush's Indiana battery suffered 3 killed and 9 wounded.[241]

The four hundred men of the 24th Illinois Infantry, who fought against Maney's 6th Tennessee and Stewart's 4th Tennessee during the Southern attack, lost 30 killed, 77 wounded and 8 missing, or 28.8 percent of its command. The 79th Pennsylvania, whose men were bloodied while grinding down Stewart's advance, entered the fight with 420 men. When the battle ended, this regiment reported 40 killed, 146 wounded and 30 missing, for an astounding loss of more than 51percent of its force. Adam S. Johnston of Company D reported that "in one hour and three quarters [the 79th Pennsylvania] lost two hundred and eleven men out of our regiment...We went into the fight with forty-three men in our company and came out with eighteen." Some family members heard of their relatives' fate in a blunt manner. After the battle, Mrs. Elizabeth Jones learned what became of her husband, who fought in the 79th Pennsylvania. Christian Matthews, a soldier in that regiment, wrote to Mrs. Jones that "Mrs. Jones, yor Husband fell in the Battle of Chaplain Heights. He was shot in the brest, he live 15 minuats until he was dead."[242]

The 1st Wisconsin, whose stand along the stone wall west of Starkweather's initial position likely saved the Union army at Perryville, suffered severely. Of the 407 members who fought at Perryville, 54 were killed, 132 were wounded and 12 were missing. Thus, the 1st Wisconsin suffered a staggering 49 percent casualties. Had these troops not made their stand behind the wall, McCook's entire corps could have been routed.[243]

Terrill's beleaguered regiments were also torn apart. Of the 2,406 men in this brigade, 112 were killed, 336 were wounded and 59 were missing. These casualties represent 22 percent of Terrill's command. Parsons' battery lost heavily. The 136 newly trained artillerymen suffered 10 killed, 19 wounded and 10 missing, or nearly 30 percent of the battery. The 659-strong 80th Illinois was the only one of Terrill's units to escape the battle relatively unscathed. In addition to having their colonel wounded, these men who formed Terrill's far-right flank on Parsons' ridge lost 15 killed and 41 wounded, or nearly 9 percent of their command. It is likely that its losses were lighter because it was one of the last of Terrill's regiments to deploy, and the brunt of Maney's attack was aimed at Parsons' battery, farther off to its left. Garrard's detachment, 194-strong, suffered a more significant loss. Garrard's 3rd Tennessee sustained 13 men wounded out of 78 engaged; his 32nd Kentucky (numbering 45 men) lost 1 killed, 5 wounded and 8 missing, including Captain Robert Taylor, who was wounded. Garrard's 75 men of the 7th Kentucky suffered 12 wounded. The 123rd Illinois, 772 strong, lost 36 killed, 118 wounded and 35 missing, nearly 25 percent of its command. Most of Terrill's casualties fell on the 105th Ohio, whose members fought Maney's Brigade throughout the day. This regiment, which consisted of 645 men, lost 50 killed, 147 wounded and 6 missing, or a loss of nearly 32 percent. Furthermore, the ratio of men killed to wounded was high for this Buckeye regiment.[244]

For the Confederates, the day's fight on the northern side of the battlefield was best described by John Magee of Stanford's Battery. Magee called it a "[b]eautiful but bloody day." Cheatham, Maney's immediate superior, was elated. He remarked that "[b]efore dark my command had possession of all the ground twelve or fifteen hundred yards to the front of where we found the enemy and held it until withdrawn during the night by orders of General Bragg."[245]

Most of Cheatham's success during the Battle of Perryville can be attributed to Maney's Brigade, which, while rushing to aid Donelson's attack, took three artillery batteries and struck the enemy at three different points: Parsons' ridge above the split-rail fence, Starkweather's initial location and Starkweather's third position, where intermingling Union brigades formed a final defense behind the stone wall. This action was arguably the zenith of the western Confederacy. Historian Kenneth W. Noe, author of *Perryville: This Grand Havoc of Battle*, noted that "[t]he high-water mark of the Confederacy in the western theater, no less important than the Angle at Gettysburg, had been reached. The Union army, as it would at Gettysburg a year later, held."[246]

Maney's Brigade suffered for the Unionists' stand. Although it forced back two strong, yet inexperienced, Federal brigades, it paid a severe price. Immediately after the battle, Maney recorded that he lost "some of the bravest and best" in his brigade. With at least 170 men killed, 502 wounded and 50 missing, Maney lost nearly 38 percent of his brigade. It was also reported that Maney was injured in the fray "when his horse kicked him on the temple."[247]

The 6th Tennessee, which entered the fight with about 315 soldiers, lost 15 killed, 66 wounded and 10 missing, or nearly 29 percent casualties. Of the 210 men of the 27th Tennessee in the fight, 20 were killed, 77 wounded and 11 missing, or 108 total. This number constitutes a total of 51.4 percent of the 27th Tennessee's force. Maney's 9th Tennessee suffered 37 killed, 127 wounded (of which 10 to 12 died after the battle) and 25 missing. One member of the 9th Tennessee's Company H said that his company, known as the Obion Avalanche, contributed to 27 percent of the regiment's entire loss. He also noted that the 9th lost 52 percent of its strength "inside of half an hour."[248]

After the war, it was reported that the 41st Georgia lost 40 percent casualties, including all of its field officers. These losses were so staggering that Maney wrote, "It may be confidently be trusted that the memory of the

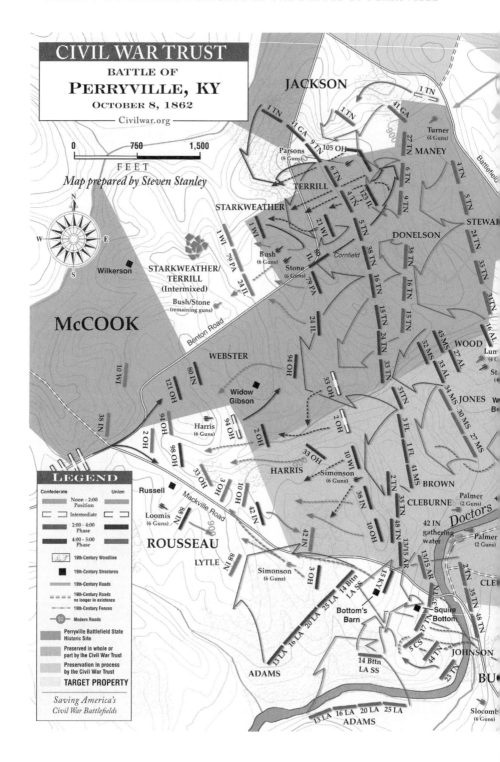

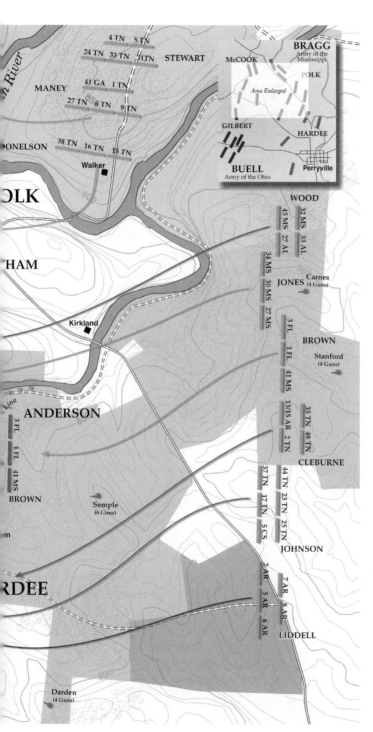

The Battle of Perryville. Maney's Brigade fought on the extreme northern end of the Confederate line. *Map courtesy of the Civil War Trust.*

field of Perryville will be a bond of future friendship and sympathy between the people of Georgia and Tennessee." The Georgians, however, initially on the far right of Maney's line, lost 42 killed, 106 wounded and 3 missing, for a total of 151 casualties, a loss of 29 percent. Within the unit, one of the hardest-hit companies was Company E, the "Troup Light Brigade," which hailed from LaGrange, Georgia. Of the 75 men in this company, 43 were killed and wounded at Perryville. Of the 4 men of Company E who served as the color guard, 1 was killed and the other 3 were severely injured. The entire regiment lost 6 men who carried the colors, with 2 killed and 4 wounded. The hazards of this duty were highlighted by the fact that the colors had six holes shot through them. So many officers were killed in this regiment that A.J. West was promoted for gallantry at Perryville. West, who was wounded during the battle, was not yet eighteen years old.[249]

"In this battle," a member of the 1st Tennessee wrote, the regiment "lost two-thirds of its men." Although this was a postwar exaggeration, the losses were severe. Entering the Battle of Perryville with about 400 men, the 1st Tennessee lost 56 killed, 122 wounded and 1 missing, or 179 total casualties. Therefore, the unit lost 45 percent of their force. Company G went into battle with 40 men, but only 13 emerged unscathed. Every officer in this company was killed or wounded, including its captain, Lute Irwin, who was severely injured.[250]

The other two brigades in Cheatham's Division, Donelson's and Stewart's, also suffered heavy casualties. Donelson lost 71 killed, 300 wounded and 3 missing, constituting 26 percent of the command. Colonel John Savage's 16th Tennessee, Donelson's regiment that was thrown out in front of the Confederate attack during the opening assault, suffered 219 casualties (nearly 60 percent of the brigade), which represents nearly two-thirds of Donelson's total loss. It is evident that the confusion of the opening phases of the battle was indeed dangerous for Donelson's men.[251]

Stewart, whose command totaled 1,466 men, lost even more soldiers. With 62 troops killed, 336 wounded and 25 missing, Stewart's casualties reached 423 men. This brigade commander lamented that he suffered "casualties which [were] very heavy for the numbers engaged, amounting I believe to over one third." Indeed Stewart lost nearly 29 percent of his brigade. W.H. Loftin of the 24th Tennessee recalled that his company, Company D, which had been reduced by sickness, went into battle with two lieutenants and seventeen enlisted men. "When the battle was over," Loftin wrote, "we had only four men left on the line, and two of them slightly wounded. The rest were killed or wounded. I was one of four left on the field, slightly wounded." Stewart's 4th and 5th Tennessee regiments were so decimated by the Battle of Perryville and the hard march of the retreat that they were consolidated shortly after the battle.[252]

Maney's Brigade was responsible for reaching the high-water mark of the western Confederacy. After routing Terrill's inexperienced brigade and driving off his artillery, the command turned against Starkweather's force, driving these veteran Unionists from hilltop to hilltop. Had Maney, assisted by Stewart, been able to continue his advance, the Confederates would have seized the Dixville Crossroads, leading to the complete rout of Union Major General Alexander McCook's corps. When the battle flag of the 1st Tennessee was captured and Maney's Brigade was forced back, however, the high tide receded. Starkweather's actions saved the Union left, sparing McCook's corps from further destruction.

These Confederates suffered some of the highest casualty percentages of any brigade that fought at Perryville. This statistic is not surprising, considering that the troops were fighting in compact lines less than one hundred yards away from one another, slugging it out from ridge to ridge. The leadership displayed by Maney's colonels—men like Hume Feild (1st Tennessee), George Porter (6th Tennessee), John Buford (wounded, 9th Tennessee), William Frierson (27th Tennessee) and Charles McDaniel (mortally wounded, 41st Georgia)—and the presence of Turner's artillery battery, coupled with the inexperience of many of the Union soldiers, allowed Maney's Brigade to find initial success. With Maney later criticized for not leading from the front, it is evident that these colonels and other officers moved the men forward when action was most needed. Their presence and determination kept the tide rolling despite horrific casualties. Bragg was correct in his post-battle assessment that "[n]obler troops were never more gallantly led."[253]

Chapter 11

"Both Whipped"

While Maney's Brigade assaulted the northern end of the Union line, Bragg's attack continued from the north to the south. Shortly after Cheatham's Division struck the Federal left flank, two brigades in Brigadier General Patton Anderson's division hit the Federal center. Colonel Thomas Marshall Jones's brigade of Mississippi and Alabama troops crossed Doctor's Creek, trudged westward across several hills and then struck two enemy infantry brigades and six cannons. Unsuccessful, Jones withdrew and was replaced by Colonel John C. Brown's brigade, but Brown's attack also failed.[254]

As the Union center held, Confederate Major General Simon Bolivar Buckner's division hit the Federal right flank, located on a hill above the Henry P. Bottom house. Confederate Brigadier General Bushrod Johnson's brigade attacked the 3rd Ohio Infantry, which was soon replaced by the 15th Kentucky Infantry. Soon, additional Rebel brigades, commanded by Brigadier Generals Patrick Cleburne and Daniel Adams, entered the fray, and the Union right flank broke.[255]

With the Union right in tatters, the center of its line collapsed, and the Federals fell back to the Dixville Crossroads, the intersection of the Benton and Mackville Roads. By 4:00 p.m., both flanks of the Union army had been shoved to the west. Although the Unionists established a temporary line at the Russell House, fresh Southern brigades commanded by Brigadier Generals S.A.M. Wood and St. John R. Liddell moved toward the crossroads.[256]

As Union troops redeployed around the Dixville Crossroads, nearly forty thousand other Federals sat idle west and south of Perryville, just a few miles

Union General Alexander McCook commanded the First Corps in the Army of the Ohio. McCook's corps bore the brunt of the Confederate attack. *Courtesy of the Library of Congress.*

from the fighting. Reinforcements were not sent in until late in the afternoon because these Northerners could not hear the battle. Because of Perryville's rolling terrain and the wind direction, a strange atmospheric phenomenon called an "acoustic shadow" blocked the sound from Union commanders west of town. Finally, at 4:00 p.m., one of McCook's aides reached Buell's headquarters. The aide informed the stunned commander that, Buell wrote, "to my astonishment, that the left corps had actually been engaged in a severe battle for several hours."[257]

As McCook's flanks collapsed, Union Colonel Michael Gooding's brigade, which had spent the day west of town, entered the fight. Upon reaching the Dixville Crossroads, Gooding's command fought Wood's soldiers before Liddell's Confederates nearly seized the intersection. Night was falling, and Union and Confederate lines, fighting just a few yards away from each other, intermingled. Gooding's brigade was torn apart at the crossroads, but with the coming darkness, the Confederates declined to press the attack. There would be no more fighting.[258]

Although the Confederate army had won a tactical victory at Perryville (it pushed back both flanks of the Union 1st Corps and killed and wounded more enemy troops), the Rebels suffered a strategic defeat. The Southerners battered the Union position north of town, but nearly forty thousand Northern troops south and west of town were not actively engaged. That night, the Confederates learned that tens of thousands of enemy troops could fight the next day. Facing these odds, Bragg withdrew to Harrodsburg, leaving the Confederate dead, and many wounded, on the battlefield. The Rebels, disappointed over a lack of recruits, eventually left Kentucky.

For the time engaged, casualties were severe. Bragg's attacking Confederates lost 532 killed, 2,641 wounded and 228 missing. Buell's Federals suffered more, with 894 killed, 2,911 wounded and 471 missing. Of these 7,677 casualties, at least 2,383 died, meaning that one out of three soldiers were either killed outright or were mortally wounded. Since the battle raged for about five hours, nearly 1,600 men were killed and injured each hour. This heavy toll illustrates why many veterans called Perryville the hardest fought and most intense battle of the Civil War.[259]

Private Sam Watkins of the 1st Tennessee was one who recognized the battle's severity. "I was in every battle, skirmish and march that was made by the First Tennessee Regiment during the war," Watkins wrote, "and I do not remember of a harder contest and more evenly fought battle than that of Perryville. If it had been two men wrestling, it would have been called a 'dog fall.' Both sides claim the victory—both whipped."[260]

The men who fought on the northern end of the battlefield suffered the heaviest casualties, with many regiments losing about 50 percent of their strength. As noted, Donelson's 16th Tennessee endured 59 percent casualties, Stewart's 4th Tennessee lost 50 percent, Maney's 9th Tennessee suffered 50 percent, Maney's 1st Tennessee lost 45 percent, his 27th Tennessee suffered 51 percent, Starkweather's 79th Pennsylvania lost 51 percent and Starkweather's 1st Wisconsin lost 49 percent. According to William T. Clark of the 79th Pennsylvania, the largest numbers of dead and wounded were found on the Union left flank.[261]

On the night of the battle, many of the Confederates initially remained on the field. Maney and Stewart's troops formed a defensive line near

Parsons' ridge, but they quickly fell back to join Donelson's Brigade. There, one drought-stricken Georgian was so thirsty that he and his comrades "drank copiously of soap suds from the wash tubs."[262]

Although the fighting was over, the field was still dangerous. Captain Edward Bowers, a minister in the 105th Ohio, held a prayer service near Starkweather's hill. Upon hearing a hymn sung, the regiment's colonel ordered the clergyman to stop the singing in case it drew enemy fire. The somber tune likely could have escaped Rebel volleys, for nightfall brought an informal truce as both sides scoured the field for wounded. Most stretcher-bearers and battlefield searchers left their weapons in camp, tempering any hostility.[263]

At least one soldier who faced Maney's Brigade took advantage of this informal truce to get out of the war. Sergeant John Dey of the 21st Wisconsin informed his superiors that he had been captured and paroled by Southern troops while searching for the wounded. Dey went to Louisville to await exchange, but several of Dey's comrades later informed regimental officers that the sergeant had approached an unarmed group of Confederates who had warned him that he would be "taken" if he neared them. Despite the warning, Dey approached the Southerners, engaged in a "low conversation," handed over his sword and secured a parole. Federal authorities hoped to court-martial Dey, Sergeant John Otto of the 21st Wisconsin wrote, because it was "a clear case of desertion under aggravating circumstances." Many were shocked by the behavior of this forty-year-old man, who was a prominent member of his community. Otto concluded, "Perhaps Sergeant Dey lost his patriotism there in the cornfield, or on the retreat and concluded to let the other boys do the fighting." Dey reported to a parole camp in Dayton, Ohio, and was exchanged in December 1862. Ordered back to his company, no one was surprised when Dey failed to appear. For this Wisconsin soldier, one battle was enough.[264]

Although most battlefield searchers were unarmed, some sporadic firing continued at dusk. When a member of Maney's 41st Georgia walked across the battlefield, he was struck in the right cheek by a spent musket ball. The shot knocked the soldier down and gave him a black eye that lasted for several weeks. Some Unionists were crack shots.[265]

For the most part, however, compassion did exist between enemy soldiers. One instance occurred after Corporal William Woodward of the 79th Pennsylvania was wounded in the left side. Shot in the chest by a musket ball, two pieces of buckshot also struck his lungs. Woodward also lost a finger and part of his ear. After lying on the battlefield for more than ten hours, "an unlikely savior" arrived. A soldier from the 41st Georgia stumbled on the injured Pennsylvanian, saw that his canteen was empty and gave him some water. Despite the drought and Woodward's apparently fatal wounds, the Southerner traded his full wooden canteen with Woodward's empty one. The Georgian said that he had purchased the canteen in Atlanta when he left for the war. Before departing, he told Woodward that "he had carried the canteen in many battles and survived." It proved to be a good token. Woodward lived through the war.[266]

Compassion was reciprocated. As night fell, Captain B.P. Steele of the 1st Tennessee lay severely wounded on the crest of Starkweather's hill. A captain from the 1st Wisconsin found Steele, "expressed his sorrow at the Confederate's condition, moved him into a comfortable position, and gave him water from a canteen." Hours before, the two enemy regiments had struggled for supremacy of the hill. In 1904, Steele searched for the generous officer through a notice in *Confederate Veteran* magazine.[267]

The informal truce allowed the Southerners to prepare for further campaigning. With arms and accoutrements scattered across the battlefield, Confederates replenished their weapons. Maney's artillery commander at Perryville, Captain William Turner, traded his two six-pounder guns for two Federal Napoleons seized on Parsons' ridge and filled his caissons with captured ammunition. Captain William Carnes's battery, which fired on Starkweather's hill from the northernmost Confederate position, also traded its damaged guns for captured Union pieces. Furthermore, Cheatham noted, "Every man of my command brought from the battle-field [the] next morning two guns (muskets) each, hoping to find transportation to haul them off with me. As our wounded filled all of our extra wagons, they were left on the ground in a line the length of the command."[268]

The Confederates also replaced their worn uniforms. One of Donelson's men stated, "We got a lot of good, warm blankets and comfortable blue suits in this fight." Later, Federal troops refused to bury Southern corpses because the secessionists had stripped Northern bodies. An angry correspondent from the *Cincinnati Daily Enquirer* reported, "Roving parties from both armies wandered over the battle-field, most of which was held by the enemy—some to look after missing friends, but more to rifle and outrage the dead...a survey of the field displayed the disgusting sight of all the dead, denuded of coats, hats, pants and shoes, and all the pockets left turned inside out. Undoubtedly most of this was done by the rebels, for the clothes they exchanged for those they had stolen, left on the field, told the tale."[269]

Although some plundered, most of the troops were on the field to remove the injured. A member of Cheatham's Division, Major J.T. Williamson of the 51st Tennessee, clearly remembered the suffering. Williamson wrote that Perryville "was the hottest fight for the time it lasted that I was in during the war. We slept right on the ground where we had made the last charge. The dead Yankees were lying thick on the ground." He added that "a pathetic scene took place that night. A Federal soldier boy was wounded and lying near where we were bivouacked. He begged piteously for his mother and to be taken away as [he feared that] the fight would be renewed the next day."[270]

The aftermath was particularly shocking to neophyte soldiers. Mead Holmes of the 21st Wisconsin helped remove the dead and injured. "The moon shone full upon the scene," Holmes detailed, "it is utterly useless to describe the sight—men and horses dead and wounded, wagon-wheels, arms, caissons scattered, and the moans and shrieks of the wounded. Oh, may you never see such a sight! I helped carry off one poor fellow with his mouth and lower jaw shot off."[271]

At dawn on October 9, Union Captain Samuel Starling, who had carried Brigadier General James S. Jackson's body away from Parsons' ridge, looked for his commander's corpse. Near the hill, Starling "found quite a number of Rebel and Union soldiers, ministering to the wounded and looking at the ground." Between these foes, Starling recalled, "all animosity had ceased and they were mixing like friends." The officer found Jackson's body, but the general's boots, hat and buttons were gone.[272]

War correspondents also inspected the battleground. A reporter from the *Louisville Journal* eyed Starkweather's hill, writing, "In Captain Stone's front I this morning saw four dead rebels who had been killed by a single shot. The top of the head of the first was taken off, the entire head of the second was gone, the breast of the third was torn open, and the ball passed through the abdomen of the [fourth]. All had fallen in a heap, killed instantly." These four corpses intrigued many witnesses and became a primary battlefield curiosity. Maney's adjutant, Thomas Malone, saw a similar scene during a nighttime visit to the battlefield. He wrote, "I remember seeing what appeared to me to be a great bundle of rags, and Emmett Cockrill and I got down to examine it. It proved to be a body in which, it seemed, a shell had exploded, leaving no trace of humanity except blood and bones and shattered flesh."[273]

Many Union soldiers were surprised that the fighting did not renew on October 9. "We were expecting a big fight today, but when daylight came the rebels were retreating," penned a perplexed member of the 80th Illinois. "I then went over the battleground and there I saw the dead and wounded lying thick. They were shot in all conceivable ways and places. It was a sickening sight to see the poor fellows a lying." Bliss Morse of the 105th Ohio was also shocked. "It is a sad sight to see dead men lay with balls shot through their heads, some with arms, legs and bowels torn off," Morse wrote. "Some lay with their tongues swelled out of their mouths, and others laid with hands stuck out as if surprised, with an expression of amusement on their faces. They were very much distorted."[274]

Most concerning for many who experienced the aftermath of the Battle of Perryville were the hogs that rooted up corpses. Before the Confederates left Perryville, they hastily created pens to protect their dead from the swine. Mead Holmes noted, "We passed a cornfield of eight acres almost covered with pens made of rails and covered with straw. These are filled with dead rebels."[275]

Sadly, there were not enough pens to protect all of the bodies. A day after the battle, a member of Rousseau's staff commented that the swine "now held possession of the field." Seven days later, another Union officer informed his wife that the battleground was "the most horrid sight that ever man beheld. Today there are hundreds of men being eaten up by the buzzards and hogs." A member of the 81st Indiana told the *New Albany Daily Ledger* that "[i]n one place lay a wounded rebel too helpless to move, and near him lay one of his dead comrades, with the top of his head torn off, and hogs eating his body—the wounded men unable to drive them away."[276]

Perryville's three hundred inhabitants, and the residents of other nearby communities, were left to bury the dead, feed the wounded and repair their farms after months of post-battle occupation. Residents' clothes were shredded for bandages; food and livestock were devoured; and fences, outbuildings and furniture were burned for firewood. Homes, businesses, churches, stables, barns and sheds became field hospitals for the thousands of wounded and sick. Residents who fled town returned to find their homes and shops full of wounded troops and their winter stores consumed.

When the 21st Wisconsin moved away from its final position, it passed a "country house" that had been converted into a hospital. There, the men found that "[t]he yard was literally covered with the wounded, dead and dying. The dead silence was broken by the most painful groans of the wounded…A few hours before they were as strong and full of hope as those who marched by them."[277]

Another member of the 21st Wisconsin, Sergeant John H. Otto, also remembered the hospitals:

> *Our brigade was moved back now ¼ of a mile and regimental details made to look after the wounded and bring them to the hospital. That sounds very big but one must not expect [too] much of a hospital behind a battlefield.*

In this case the hospitals consisted of a few small houses in Perryville, two small log barns in the rear of the battlefield and one big hospital tent. The barn nearest to the line was used as an amputation room; that is [where] arms and legs were sawed off. The boys called it the "butcher shop" or "barnyard." [O]thers gave it the very proper name of "Uncle Sam[']s Sawmill." The other barn was used or intended for the more slightly wounded. Probing for bullets and dressing of wounds was mainly performed here. As soon as they were tended to they were put out doors on the ground, covered with a blanket and left to themselfes [sic] to indulge in wholesome meditations over the beauties of patriotism and liberty; but such who were able to endure transportation in an ambulance were directly sent back to hospital in Louisville.[278]

Union surgeons were overwhelmed by the many casualties, the condition of the hospitals and the lack of medical supplies. According to Dr. J.G. Hatchitt, there were so few supplies that surgeons "were compelled to amputate without chloroform." In addition, the drought caused sanitation problems. "Some surgeons told me that they could not get water enough to wash the blood from their hands for two days," Hatchitt wrote. With no water to clean hands or instruments, deaths from post-injury infections were common. Bliss Morse of the 105th Ohio informed his mother that "Lucius Prouty died Sunday after having his leg amputated near the hip. He laid on the field one night, and day, after the fight. The Rebels gave him water while he laid on the field." There were scores of similar stories.[279]

Chapter 12

"Lay Him Down and Let Him Die"

For Maney's Brigade and the Union soldiers who fought it, two of the main field hospitals were Antioch Church, which housed Union patients, and the Goodnight farm, which held wounded from Cheatham's Division. Perryville doctor J.J. Polk recalled that "[f]or more than ten days after the battle the field hospitals, except Antioch Church and Mr. Goodnight's farm, were being cleared of the wounded; the two above excepted contained about three hundred of the wounded."[280]

Many of the injured from Terrill's and Starkweather's brigades were taken to Antioch Church, located north of the battleground in Mercer County. Adam Johnston of the 79th Pennsylvania, who had been shot below his left knee, was one of these soldiers. After lying on the field for a day, Johnston was taken to the church, where he and three others were "thrown out in a pile like wood… the church was perfectly filled and [wounded were] under ever shade tree nigh at hand…I lay for six days out under a white oak tree, with my wound dressed once." Johnston's experiences are illustrative of what other men in his brigade endured. On October 15, he was moved from the church to a hospital within the city limits of Perryville. Eight days later, he traveled fifteen miles southward to Lebanon, where he stayed for four more days. Transported to Louisville, Johnston entered a hospital at New Albany, Indiana, on November 6. Finally, on January 9, 1863, the soldier left to rejoin his regiment.[281]

Lieutenant John Hartzell of the 105th Ohio stumbled on Antioch Church. He wrote that "[t]he church was full of poor, mangled fellows. Surgeons were busy, and piles of naked and bloody limbs, hands, feet, legs and arms lay about the church." Several of the men who faced Maney's Brigade died at the house of worship. These included Private Albert Richardson of the 80th Illinois and Private George Newsome of the 123rd Illinois, who died from his wounds on October 29. From that same regiment, Private John Lawrence passed away on October 22, while Private James Pruett died five days after the battle. Private Jerome Smith of the 105th Ohio died at the church on the day of the battle, and the nineteen-year-old Buckeye Private John Tucker passed away on October 13. Men from Starkweather's units, including Corporal Aaron Sherwood of the 21st Wisconsin, also lost their lives there. Initially buried on site, their remains now rest at Camp Nelson National Cemetery in Jessamine County.[282]

Cheatham's wounded, including Maney's injured, were left at the Goodnight farm, about one mile east of the battlefield. According to Cheatham, many of his wounded were loaded into wagons to travel with the retreating army, but most of these troops were left in Harrodsburg, ten miles from the battlefield. Cheatham added that "the balance were left in the old house [Goodnight] and in fence-corners. Dr. [J.R.] Buist was left in charge of them, [and] he built shelters over them with brush and corn-stalks to keep the sun off." Like the Northern troops, the wounded Confederates endured miserable conditions.[283]

Sam Watkins was one of the soldiers who helped transport his injured comrades to the Goodnight farm. "We helped bring off a man by the name of Hodge," Watkins wrote, "with his under jaw shot off and his tongue lolling out. We brought off Captain Lute B. [Irwin]. Lute was shot though the lungs and was vomiting blood all the while, and begging us to lay him down and let him die. But Lute is living yet. Also, Lieutenant [Woldridge], with both eyes shot out. I found him rambling in a briar patch."[284]

Surprisingly, Watkins's patients survived. One, Lewis "Lute" Broyles Irwin, was a well-respected physician who enlisted in Company G of Maney's 1st Tennessee Infantry in the spring of 1861. While campaigning in western Virginia, he was elected captain. Severely wounded at Perryville, Lute was, according to his obituary, left at the Goodnight farm "with hundreds of other wounded to be surrendered to the enemy. Their bed was straw spread upon the ground in a lot inclosed [sic] with a rail fence, their covering the canopy of heaven, which constituted the field hospital." Irwin recovered and returned to the regiment but was unfit to serve in the field. He spent the rest of the war "assigned to post duty." Perryville ended his fighting career.[285]

When Watkins penned his memoirs forty years after the battle, Lute was "living yet." Irwin returned to his medical practice and died on September

29, 1909, at the age of seventy-five years and seven months. He was assuredly thankful that Watkins did not "lay him down and let him die."[286]

Watkins and Marcus Toney of Company B, 1st Tennessee, were both surprised that the fifteen-year-old Billy Whitthorne, shot through the neck while charging Starkweather's hill, also survived the battle. Toney expected to bury him that night, but they never found his body. Instead, the boy had simply walked off the field. Whitthorne's combat experiences continued long past his childhood. He fought in the Spanish-American War and eventually became a major in the U.S. Army. Another amazing tale of survival was that of Captain Dick Steele, the twenty-six-year-old captain of Company A, 1st Tennessee. Like Whitthorne, Steele was grievously wounded while charging Starkweather's position. Treated at the Goodnight house by Toney, Steele's obituary noted, "He never recovered fully from the wounds, but for nearly half a century suffered cheerfully."[287]

Watkins also aided Lieutenant John H. Woldridge. Born in Pulaski, Tennessee, on September 20, 1836, Woldridge was educated at Lynnville, Tennessee, and Giles College in Pulaski. Woldridge graduated from law school in Lebanon, Tennessee, in 1858 and then joined a private law practice. Upon the outbreak of the Civil War, he and his law partner enlisted in the 1st Tennessee Infantry. Woldridge fought with the unit throughout western Virginia and, at Perryville, led Company K. During the regiment's charge up Starkweather's hill, the officer was shot through the temple. The bullet severed his optic nerve, blinding him in both eyes.[288]

Ethel Moore was a young woman who traveled with Cheatham's Division during much of the war, including the Perryville Campaign. In 1898, while addressing a group of Southern veterans, she recalled Woldridge's sad predicament. "Well do I remember," she said, "after spending all night on the battlefield gathering up the wounded of Cheatham's Division and sending them to the rear, coming at daylight and going back to the Goodnight hospital, some three miles in the rear, finding Lieut. Woldridge lying on the floor with a cloth over the upper part of his face, the sight from both eyes gone forever to this world." Moore, and many of Woldridge's fellow soldiers, believed the wound to be mortal. The blind soldier survived, and after the war, a Confederate Veterans' Bivouac in Giles County, Tennessee, was named in his honor. Blind for nearly fifty-one years, Woldridge died on July 22, 1913. According to his obituary, "He exhibited wonderful courage and endurance in his long battle over half a century against the encroachments of this terrible wound. It finally invaded his brain and caused his death." Thus, the Battle of Perryville claimed a final victim in the twentieth century.[289]

In addition to Ethel Moore, other women traveled with the Confederates during the Kentucky Campaign. Perhaps the hardiest of the lot was Mrs. Betsy Sullivan, who was known to Maney's Brigade as "Mother Sullivan." Her husband, John, was an Irish immigrant who served in Company K of the 1st Tennessee. Betsy's endurance was stellar, having marched with the regiment since the beginning of the war. According to Tennessean W.W. Cunningham, Mrs. Sullivan, who was in her early thirties at the time of the battle, "was tall and weighed about one hundred and eighty pounds." While the regiment waited in the squalor of Corinth before moving toward the Bluegrass State, Company K, which Mrs. Sullivan referred to as "her company," gave her a horse, which she rode into Kentucky.[290]

When John Sullivan charged Starkweather's position, he received "a hole in his forehead that exposed a part of the brain" and was left for dead on the field. At midnight, Betsy Sullivan, waiting at the Goodnight house, learned that her husband had been shot. Alone, she took to the field to find him and returned to the Goodnight farm several hours later. According to Toney, Betsy "was a stalwart woman, and brought John on her shoulder to the hospital." John recovered under Betsy's meticulous care, and two weeks later, the Sullivans and the blind Woldridge procured a "carryall" to travel to Pulaski, Tennessee. Near Lebanon, Kentucky, however, Union authorities captured the party and sent them to prison. While some sources state that Mrs. Sullivan was incarcerated with her husband, she likely went home to Pulaski to await his return. When John was exchanged and rejoined the regiment, Betsy visited him. Although her disabled husband could not return to the field, Mrs. Sullivan wanted to remain with the regiment. The 1st Tennessee refused, but to thank her for her arduous service, it raised a large sum as a gift. According to Cunningham, the troops gave her $25,000.[291]

While most of the Confederates left Perryville after the battle, a handful of Rebels remained behind to care for their wounded comrades. In Maney's Brigade, Private Marcus Toney of the 1st Tennessee performed arduous service in assisting the injured from his regiment. Like Watkins, Toney spent the night of the battle searching for friends. "It was a sad sight that night as I gazed upon the upturned, ghastly faces of our dead," Toney wrote, "and the cries of the wounded for 'water!' 'water!' 'water!' was heartrending."[292]

Toney's experiences at Perryville also illustrate the "brother against brother" nature of the Civil War in Kentucky. Upon reaching Starkweather's hill, Toney found dozens of dead from his regiment. His company had lost fourteen killed and thirteen wounded while charging the Union guns. Among the dead was one of Toney's "intimate friends," Robert S. Hamilton. A native

Kentuckian who worked as a proofreader in Nashville, Hamilton joined the 1st Tennessee at age eighteen. Although Hamilton's Bluegrass family was divided over the war, Robert was an avid secessionist. During one of the final charges up Starkweather's hill, he was shot in the forehead and killed.

Toney knew that Hamilton had relatives in Lexington, fifty miles from the battlefield. From the light of a burning barn, Toney wrote to Hamilton's sister-in-law, Mrs. Wesley C. Hamilton, a simple note: "Robert was killed in [a] gallant charge this evening. Will take care of [his] remains until you arrive." Toney did not write to Robert's brother because Wesley "was a Union man, and Robert never wrote a line to him; but all his correspondence was with his sister-in-law." A Union soldier agreed to deliver the note to Mrs. Hamilton.[293]

That night, Toney buried twenty-seven members of the 1st Tennessee in a gully behind Starkweather's hill. Using a Federal breastplate (an ornamental device), he scooped dirt over the corpses, burying Hamilton at the head of the line. Of those known to have been buried there, seven were from Company A, fourteen were from Company B and one was from Company C.[294]

Toney returned to the Goodnight farm, where he cared for eight wounded comrades, including the blind Woldridge and Lute Irwin. Their wounds were severe enough to be remembered by Toney, Sam Watkins and Charles Quintard, the chaplain of the 1st Tennessee. Toney exclaimed that "Woldridge lost both of his eyes" and that Irwin was "badly wounded." Nursing them at the Goodnight house proved to be strenuous. "For three nights," he wrote, "I did not close my eyes in sleep." Quintard also worked diligently, recalling that from 3:00 p.m. "until half past five the next morning, without food of any sort, I was incessantly occupied with the wounded. It was a horrible night I spent—God save me from such another. I suppose excitement kept me up. About half past five in the morning of the 9th, I dropped—I could do no more. I went out by myself and leaning against a fence, I wept like a child. And all that day I was so unnerved that if any one asked me about the regiment [1st Tennessee], I could make no reply without tears. Having taken off my shirt to tear into strips to make bandages, I took a severe cold."[295]

On October 11, Mrs. Hamilton arrived from Lexington with a hearse and casket for her deceased brother-in-law. She also brought blankets and food for the wounded Confederates. Toney guided her across the Goodnight farm, past the Walker house and over the corpse-strewn battlefield. When they reached Starkweather's hill, Toney stopped at the mass grave and raked the dirt away from Robert's face. "Mrs. Hamilton," the Confederate said, "this is Robert."

With Robert disfigured from the wound and decomposition, Mrs. Hamilton was shocked at the sight. She asked, "Is it possible that these are Robert's remains?" To persuade her, Toney lifted one of Robert's hands from the ground. Brushing the dirt away, Toney displayed Robert's fingers. Apparently, whenever Robert was deep in thought, he bit his fingernails, chewing them so short that he drew blood. When Mrs. Hamilton saw the fingers, she recognized her brother-in-law's remains, thanked Toney, and returned to Lexington with his body. Robert was interred at the Lexington Cemetery, where he is the only known Confederate casualty from the Battle of Perryville.[296]

Robert was killed by Federal troops, but his family still supported the Union cause. Robert's brother, John W. Hamilton, joined the 18th Kentucky (Union) Infantry Regiment in March 1864. Therefore, nearly two years after Robert was killed by Federal troops, his brother enlisted in the Union army. John survived the war but died in 1867 at age thirty-seven. Both brothers, who fought on opposing sides, are interred in the Hamilton family plot in Section C, Lot 16 of the Lexington Cemetery. Standing at the plot is a moving experience as one envisions the family's familial divisions. The bottom of Robert's grave lists "CSA," while John's headstone is inscribed "USA." These two brothers, who fought on opposite sides, are now united in burial. They served different causes but share the same ground.[297]

Thanks to the work of soldier-nurses like Toney, some of the wounded Confederates at the Goodnight farm survived. One fortunate soldier was Lieutenant James I. Hall of the 9th Tennessee. After Hall's regiment captured Parsons' Battery, the Tennessean was wounded in the torso. He lay on the battlefield all evening and was taken to the Goodnight farm near midnight. He later wrote:

The surgeons, on examination, pronounced my wound necessarily mortal and I was placed on the ground under an apple tree between two men whose wounds were similar to mine. A liberal dose of morphine was given to each one of us and I remember its soothing effect on me. The other two men were suffering intensely from their wounds and knowing that my wound was similar to theirs kept me awake for a long time by asking me such questions as "how I felt" and "whether I thought I could last through the night." I finally got to sleep and when I awoke the next morning, I had a corpse at each elbow. The men had died while I slept. Contrary to the predictions of the surgeons, I was still alive.[298]

Hall remained outside for several days, his condition exacerbated because his clothes had been ripped away by the doctors who examined his wound. Exposed to the elements, he was eventually placed under a lean-to made from old planks. The shelter helped, he wrote, because "a heavy snow fell greatly to the discomfort of our men in the hospital, since they weren't all provided with shelter and clothing. A large number of our men, however, were taken to the homes of the good people in the country in Harrodsburg and Danville." Immediately after the battle, citizens from the region traveled to the hospitals and distributed food, clothing and blankets. Southern sympathizer Florence Goalder and her sister, for example, both from Green County, Kentucky, scoured their area for supplies and rode forty miles to deliver them to wounded Confederates.[299]

Hall remained at the Goodnight farm for about two weeks. Surprisingly, this Rebel's savior was a Unionist. Colonel Joshua Barbee of Danville sent his carriage to Perryville and retrieved Hall, who knew the family. Hall had boarded at Barbee's home, a Greek Revival mansion on the east end of Danville, when he was a student at Centre College. Taken to Barbee's residence, Hall wrote that he was "placed in the room which I had occupied fifteen years earlier while a student at Centre College and was treated with unremitting kindness by Colonel B. and his family."[300]

Hall remained there for more than two months. Finally, after pulling strings with former Centre College classmates, Hall secured a parole for himself and several wounded comrades. His return surprised his loved ones. Hall's wound had been pronounced mortal, and newspapers and official reports noted that the officer had died. The lieutenant's family read about his demise in the newspapers. Later, Hall recalled, his family and friends

> had no hope of ever seeing me again. The only one who seemed inclined to discredit the report was my six year old daughter who could not be convinced that I was dead and would say to her grandmother: "Grandma, Papa's not dead. He'll come home one of these days, now you'll see." When I finally reached home, arriving there in the dusk of evening, I found her standing alone on the porch—seemingly waiting for me. Her greeting was: "why here's Papa," and then to her Aunt Sarah, "I told you he would come back."[301]

Most children of the missing were not so fortunate. There were hundreds of families who never knew what became of their fathers, sons and brothers. Several rows of unknown men buried in Harrodsburg, Camp Nelson, Danville, Lebanon and other communities attest to this fact. More unknown dead are listed on the Confederate monument that stands over the mass grave at the Perryville Battlefield State Historic Site. As late as 1900, a note in the December issue of *Confederate Veteran* read, "Mrs. W.M. Ritchey, of Athlone, Cal., seeks information on her brother, Isaac Cunningham, who was lost in the battle of Perryville." It is likely that Mrs. Cunningham never learned of Isaac's fate, although her sadness and curiosity had lingered for nearly forty years.[302]

Like James Hall, other members of Maney's Brigade survived their wounds and the battle's aftermath. Private Edward Elam of the 9th Tennessee had his leg amputated after the battle and lived until 1881. Another member of the regiment, Private Alford Ward, lost his right leg, and he, too, survived. A third soldier in the 9th, Private George McDill, was shot through the lungs and lived until 1898. Just as miraculous is the story of Captain John M. Taylor of the 27th Tennessee. Taylor received four wounds at Perryville. Shot through both thighs, his right femur was shattered, and he was disabled for life. Taylor became a judge and lived for many more years. One of the most intriguing tales of survival, however, involved the twenty-one-year-old Robert T. Bond of the 9th Tennessee. Bond had been wounded at the Battle of Shiloh. At Perryville, he was wounded six times and survived. He eventually rejoined the command and was again injured while fighting near Atlanta. Despite eight wounds received in Confederate service, Bond survived the war.[303]

With the Confederate army having left Perryville, Union troops pressed forward the day after the battle, arrived at the Goodnight farm, and cared for the wounded Confederates left there. John Martin of the 8th Kansas Infantry described the scene. "As we pressed on evidences of a hasty flight were manifest," Martin wrote. "Their dead and wounded were left uncared for, and the ground was covered with guns, blankets and knapsacks, indicating the confusion in which they had fled." Unionist Wilbur Hinman likely visited this area when he wrote that

lying upon the ground, with no shelter from the fierce heat of the sun by day or the dew by night, were some three hundred rebel wounded. They had as yet received no care from the surgeons. Many of them were in the most horrible condition that the mind can conceive. Some were shot through the head, body or limbs, others mangled by fragments of shell, and all suffering the greatest torments. We gave them water, and shared with them the contents of our haversacks, but there was nothing else that we could do. Words are powerless to convey an adequate idea of these harrowing scenes.

Several weeks after the battle, the field hospital was closed, and the remaining wounded were sent to Harrodsburg or Danville. Of the unknown number of Confederates who died from their wounds at the Goodnight farm, most were buried at the Goodnight family cemetery. After the war, the Federal government erected a monument to the unknown dead buried there. As these Southerners were Rebel prisoners of war when they died, the Federal government recognized their passing with the monument.[304]

Despite the horrors of the aftermath, a handful of men found happiness. Two soldiers from Maney's 9th Tennessee, Willie Holmes and James Peter, were wounded during the battle. After spending time recovering at the Goodnight farm, they were sent to the house of a Mr. Messick in Danville. Here, Willie Holmes met a Miss More, whom he eventually married. Another member of the brigade, Daniel Risdon Smith of Company C, 27th Tennessee, also found local love. Like Toney, Smith remained behind to care for his wounded comrades at the Goodnight farm. According to his pension file, Smith "was absolutely the last Confederate soldier who was at the Goodknight [sic] hospital." While in Perryville, Smith met and married Minerva Bugg. He never returned to the Confederate army. The couple lived in nearby Dixville for the rest of their lives, and some of their descendants reside in the area to this day.[305]

Captain H.C. Irby of the 9th Tennessee had a similar story, but he returned to the army. At Perryville, Irby was "severely wounded and left on the field." Elizabeth F. Eubank found him at a field hospital (probably the Goodnight house) and took him home, "where she nursed him back to health and strength." Later, "when he was fully recovered they were married, and Captain Irby rejoined his command."[306]

While many wounded Confederates stayed at the Goodnight farm and other local hospitals, those who could travel followed the Army of the Mississippi the ten miles to Harrodsburg. Ultimately, at least 1,700 injured and sick, including members of Maney's Brigade, remained in Harrodsburg under the care of the town's 1,700 inhabitants.[307]

When the Federals reached Harrodsburg, wounded soldiers and Confederate nurses became prisoners of war. Hospital steward George Crosby and Private A. McMillan of the 9th Tennessee, for example, were captured there on October 11. Dozens of Confederates died in Harrodsburg, including Private J.M. Smith of the 9th Tennessee, who lingered for four months before passing away on January 10, 1863. Many of these mortally wounded Rebels were buried at the town's Springhill Cemetery. Most of the graves simply read, "Unknown." A handful of other members of Maney's

The grave of C.N. Kerr, 9th Tennessee Infantry, located at Bellevue Cemetery in Danville, Kentucky. Wounded at Perryville, Kerr died of his injury at Bryantsville, Kentucky, as the Confederate army retreated from Perryville. His remains were later moved to Danville. *Courtesy of the author.*

Brigade are buried in Danville, ten miles east of the battlefield. These include T. Harmon of the 41st Georgia and Captain C.N. Kerr of the 9th Tennessee, who died in Bryantsville.[308]

When the Confederates left Perryville, Union soldiers buried their dead in regimental plots on the field. In many instances, they gathered the bodies, wrapped them in blankets and buried them in shallow ditches. Because of the dry, rocky soil, some of the graves were only eighteen inches deep.[309]

Lieutenant John Hartzell, who oversaw the burials of the 105th Ohio, described the field and the process:

Ambulances were everywhere, gathering up their ghastly, groaning freight, twisting, turning and backing to avoid running over the dead wholly about in all sorts of shapes and places, often in groups of half a dozen, all blackened and swollen. Arrived at the lane [Benton Road, near where

133

the 105th Ohio had fought], *we located a trench, and, while some dug, others bore the bodies and laid them on the margin. It was almost impossible to go to a proper depth, the ground being so dry and hard, so we concluded on* [burying them] *two feet* [deep]. *It was very hard to identify even our own men, though we did the best we could, and as we laid the bodies in the trench, spread the limbs of each wide apart, resting the head of each on another, covering the whole with blankets, then with earth. Forty-two were in that trench, I think. It was a sad business, anyway.*[310]

In November 1862, James D. Kennedy traveled to Perryville to retrieve the body of his son, who was killed while fighting with the 105th Ohio. Upon touring the battlefield, Kennedy concluded that these soldiers "have not that decent burial their friends expect or desire." Therefore, Kennedy wrote a letter to the *Western Reserve Chronicle* in order to educate the community about the mass grave that contained the regiment's casualties and to provide assistance to families who wanted to exhume their loved ones. In graphic detail, Kennedy outlined the best time to retrieve the corpses and suggested a vendor who sold good coffins. Two weeks prior to Kennedy's message, the newspaper published a letter from a member of the regiment who wrote, "The dead were buried in trenches, and rude head boards carved with the initials of their names." Using these grave markers, Kennedy recorded the soldiers' names in the order in which they were buried, a list that he included in the letter to his community. He had faced tremendous difficulties in locating his son's remains. Therefore, he wanted to ease the burden for other parents who wanted to exhume their sons, all of whom were killed by Maney's Brigade.[311]

Kennedy wrote that "[t]he bodies are near the surface of the ground and but slightly covered, consequently they are in a measure exposed to the action of the atmosphere, therefore in the course of a fortnight they become in a putrid state, which is the most offensive, after remaining in this state about a week they begin to dry up and shrivel, so that in the course of four or five weeks after burial there is but little left on the bodies except the skin, ligaments &c., and are more dry, hard and firm, consequently very much less offensive." He added that "[n]early all of the 105th who were killed on the field are buried in a long trench just wide enough to admit two bodies side by side and lying lengthwise, two bodies are first laid in, then two more with their heads to the feet of the first and so on."[312]

Kennedy related that some casualties had already been moved from the field. Because the Battle of Perryville was fought in the border state

An 1885 image of the Confederate mass grave at the Perryville battlefield. *Courtesy of the Perryville Battlefield State Historic Site.*

of Kentucky, it was geographically closer to midwestern states than other battles. Therefore, soldiers' families could more easily reach their wounded relatives or travel to disinter their slain loved ones. However, the civilians' exhumations brought much complaint. One newspaper lamented that if families dug up the wrong grave, they were lax in reburying the bodies. As the *New Albany Daily Ledger* explained, "From this cause the remains of the dead are left exposed; here an arm, there a leg, and again a head with its ghastly face, from which the rotten flesh is dropping, and upon all which the hogs feed at will. The thought of such things is of itself horrible; its realization terrible in the extreme. No more civilians should be allowed to open graves upon the battle-field…such scenes of desecration upon its sacred soil are outrages which should never be tolerated."[313]

Although Federal corpses were quickly buried, dead Southerners lay on the field for days. For the most part, when Bragg's army departed, it left its dead where they fell. There were, however, some Southern burials immediately after

Union Brigadier General James S. Jackson was the highest-ranking Federal officer to be killed at the Battle of Perryville. *Courtesy of the Kentucky Historical Society.*

the fight. On the night of the battle, eight to ten Rebel corpses were buried "under the supervision of a Confederate colonel." According to newspaper reporter Alf Burnett, most of the Rebels were not buried until Federal authorities (spurred on by the U.S. Sanitary Commission) ordered Southern sympathizers to inter them. Another Union soldier, Private Jonathan McElderry of the 121st Ohio Infantry, stated that the dead still lay on the field five days after the battle. McElderry and others impressed slaves to finish the burials, and two to three wagonloads of corpses were hauled into a nearby cave or sinkhole. In most instances, Federal burials of Confederate dead simply consisted of "digging a deep hole beside the corpse, and the diggers, taking a couple of fence rails, would pry the body over and let it fall in the bottom."[314]

The corpse of Union Brigadier General James S. Jackson, the highest-ranking officer killed at Perryville, received the most attention. When the battle began, Maney's men shot Jackson twice in the chest as he stood near Parsons' cannons. The general's body was immediately dragged behind the artillery. The next morning, Union officers Samuel Starling and Percival Oldershaw returned to the battlefield to recover Jackson's corpse.

Because Jackson was the highest-ranking casualty, Starling and Oldershaw placed the corpse in an ambulance and left for Louisville. Upon reaching Mackville, they "got a large box & a barrel of salt [and] washed him & put him into it." They continued on, stopping briefly in Springfield to rest before

Of the Perryville residents who suffered from the aftermath of the battle, perhaps none endured more than Henry P. Bottom, pictured here at age ninety. As a result of the fight, Bottom lost nine cows, thirty sheep, thousands of pounds of pork and bacon, 1,300 panels of worm fencing, 3,020 bushels of corn, twenty-two tons of hay, 50 bushels of oats and two horses. Bottom also buried many of the Confederate dead. This included a large number from Maney's Brigade. *Courtesy of the Perryville Battlefield State Historic Site.*

The Confederate mass grave at the Perryville Battlefield State Historic Site includes a monument and a handful of individual markers. Hundreds of dead Confederates are buried in two pits in the enclosure. Most of the men buried there are unknown casualties. *Courtesy of the Perryville Battlefield State Historic Site.*

moving to Bardstown, where they telegraphed Louisville for a carriage and hearse, which met them at Mount Washington.

The party reached Louisville at 9:00 a.m. on October 11. Jackson's body lay in state at the Galt House Hotel for a day and was then, Starling wrote, "put into a large metallic box (not coffin) & the next day was taken to Christs [sic] Church where on entering several Ladies threw wreaths of flowers upon it." Reverend Jeremiah Talbott gave a eulogy, and then an infantry regiment escorted the body to Cave Hill Cemetery. After a salute was fired, Jackson was placed in a vault. This Federal officer was later reinterred in Hopkinsville, where he had established a law practice and political career prior to the war.[315]

Dead Southerners received less pomp and circumstance. Many of them were buried by Henry P. Bottom, a local farmer who owned most of the land on which the battle was fought. Gathering the bodies in the area where he found the most corpses (where Cheatham's Division had attacked on the northern end of the battleground), Bottom and his field hands interred several hundred Confederates in two large pits. Although Bottom tried to identify many of the dead, more than four hundred of the soldiers listed on the monument placed over the mass grave remain unknown.[316]

According to a Mackville resident, after Bottom buried the bodies, he "cut initials in a shingle and put [the board] over them where they buried them." By 1897, the mass grave was, according to one veteran, "entirely grown up in briers and weeds, and is the picture of desolation." Only one grave, one of Maney's men, was marked. Placed by the soldier's wife, it read, "Sam H. Ransom, First Tennessee Regiment, C.S.A., October 8, 1862—age, twenty-seven. 'Our parting is not forever.'" By 1900, the ground was still "grown up in weeds and bushes," and Ransom's grave was still the only marked plot. By this time, however, the stone had broken off at the base. In 1902, the Commonwealth of Kentucky built a stone wall around the grave and erected a monument inscribed with verses from Danville native Theodore O'Hara's poem, "Bivouac of the Dead." The mass grave is now preserved at the Perryville Battlefield State Historic Site. Buried therein, their names now forgotten, are many men from Maney's Brigade.[317]

EPILOGUE

While many of Maney's regiments suffered nearly 50 percent casualties at Perryville, their commander survived the battle and the Civil War. Despite having some subordinates question his bravery and actions at Perryville—notably remaining at the fence with the reserve while his front line advanced—Maney continued to command a brigade in the Confederate army. Maney fought at Murfreesboro, Chickamauga and Chattanooga, where he was wounded. Sent to Atlanta to heal, his performance at Perryville came back to haunt his recuperation. One of the general's obituaries stated that "[a]fter his arrival at Atlanta he fought his historic duel with Dr. William Nichol, of Nashville, a surgeon in the Confederate army...Maney ascertained that Dr. Nichol had impugned his motives as a soldier by stating that he was not at the head of his regiment at the battle of Perryville, and challenged Dr. Nichol. The latter was wounded during the encounter."[318]

Having defended his honor and recovered from his wound, Maney led Cheatham's Division during part of the Atlanta Campaign, fighting with it at Peach Tree Creek and Jonesborough. By August 31, 1864, however, he had been given "a leave of absence on a surgeon's certificate of disability." While that effectively ended his service, he may have concluded the war as an aide to Major General William Hardee.[319]

The charges of failing to do his duty at Perryville may have dogged Maney's chances for promotion. Although he was recommended for advancement on multiple occasions, he remained a brigadier general. In one instance, Hardee, who saw Maney fight at Perryville and Murfreesboro, noted that

Confederate Major General William Hardee. Maney may have ended his Civil War service as an aide to this general, who commanded a wing at the Battle of Perryville. *Courtesy of the Kentucky Historical Society.*

"his intelligence, force of character, and military experience, are such as eminently fit him for the command of a Division." No promotion, however, was forthcoming.[320]

After the war, Maney was a lawyer in Nashville and became president of the Tennessee & Pacific Railroad. Surprisingly, Maney also became a Republican and stridently worked to strengthen the party of Lincoln in Tennessee. In 1881, President James Garfield named him minister to Columbia. Maney later served as minister to Bolivia, as a state senator in Tennessee and as "minister plenipotentiary and envoy extraordinary to Paraguay and Uruguay."[321]

Called "the flower of Tennessee chivalry," Maney died of "apoplexy" in Washington, D.C., on February 7, 1901. He was seventy-five. His body was shipped back to Nashville, where he was buried.[322]

Although Maney's leadership at Perryville was questioned, his brigade performed ably. In addition to the fighting spirit of his men, credit for his brigade's success can be attributed to regimental officers, aides and company commanders. If Maney caused a leadership vacuum at Perryville, those officers filled it. Men like Colonel Hume Feild, Colonel George Porter, Captain Thomas Malone and innumerable others pushed the troops forward at critical times. Many of these officers—including Lieutenant Colonel John Patterson, Colonel Charles McDaniel and more—paid the ultimate price for their conspicuous service among the hills, cornfields and fence rails of Perryville.

The élan of these officers is perhaps best illustrated by the performance of Captain George N. Lester of the 41st Georgia. According to Lester's compiled service record, the captain suffered a severe injury at Perryville when "he was wounded in the right fore-arm by a minnie [*sic*] ball, which so shattered the bones, lacerated the flesh, and severed the artery, as that the limb had to be forthwith amputated. His arm was taken off above the elbow, as the wound involved the elbow joint." Despite the horrific nature of this injury, the captain remained determined to boost the troops' morale. As the Southern columns marched from the battlefield, "Lester stood on the gallery of the hospital by the roadside, and shook hands with each member of his regiment as they passed by, and spoke words of encouragement to them."[323]

Leaders like this led Maney's Brigade through overwhelming adversity during Kentucky's largest Civil War battle. These officers, however, recognized the troops. As Colonel George Porter of the 6th Tennessee contended, "In this fight there were so many instances of individual prowess and bravery that I find it no easy task to make proper discrimination in the matter. As far as I could judge they all did their duty well and deserve the highest praise."[324]

NOTES

Chapter 1

1. Author's conversation with Helen Dedman, May 2005; "St. Philips on National Historic List," undated newspaper clipping, Perryville Battlefield Preservation Association files, Perryville, Kentucky.
2. Reverend Arthur Howard Noll, ed., *Doctor Quintard: Chaplain CSA and Second Bishop of Tennessee* (Sewanee, TN: University Press, 1905), 61–62.
3. Sam R. Watkins, *"Co. Aytch": Maury Grays First Tennessee Regiment* (Wilmington, NC: Broadfoot Publishing Company, 1990; originally published 1881–82), 71, 75.
4. Christopher Losson, *Tennessee's Forgotten Warriors: Frank Cheatham and His Confederate Division* (Knoxville: University of Tennessee Press, 1989), 60; W.D. Pickett, "Reminiscences of Murfreesoboro," *Confederate Veteran* 16 (September 1908): 449; John W. Carroll, *Autobiography and Reminiscences of John W. Carroll* (Henderson, TN, n.d.), 23.
5. Grady McWhiney, "Controversy in Kentucky: Braxton Bragg's Campaign of 1862," *Civil War History* 6 (1960): 9; Thomas Lawrence Connelly, *Army of the Heartland: The Army of Tennessee, 1861–1862* (Baton Rouge: Louisiana State University Press, 1967), 189; Gerald J. Prokopowicz, *All for the Regiment: The Army of the Ohio, 1861–1862* (Chapel Hill: University of North Carolina Press, 2001), 118; Stephen D. Engle, *Don Carlos Buell: Most Promising of All* (Chapel Hill: University of North Carolina Press, 1999),

254; Larry J. Daniel, *Days of Glory: The Army of the Cumberland, 1861–1865* (Baton Rouge: Louisiana State University Press), 86.

6. James Lee McDonough, *War in Kentucky: From Shiloh to Perryville* (Knoxville: University of Tennessee Press, 1994), 39–40; Connelly, *Army of the Heartland*, 188, 190–191; Kenneth W. Noe, *Perryville: This Grand Havoc of Battle* (Lexington: University Press of Kentucky, 2001), 24; Daniel, *Days of Glory*, 86; Thomas L. Connelly, *Civil War Tennessee* (Knoxville: University of Tennessee Press, 1979), 8–9, 11; Earl J. Hess, *Banners to the Breeze: The Kentucky Campaign, Corinth, and Stones River* (Lincoln: University of Nebraska Press, 2000), 7; Lincoln quoted in George Constable, ed., *The Time-Life History of the Civil War* (New York: Barnes and Noble Books, 1995), 298; Bragg quote from U.S. War Department, *The War of the Rebellion: A Compilation of the Official Records of the Union and Confederate Armies*, vol. 16, pt. 1 (Washington, D.C.: U.S. Government Printing Office, 1880–1901), 1089 (hereafter cited as *OR*; unless noted, all references refer to series I).

7. *OR*, vol. 16, pt. 2, 695, 709; Smith is also quoted in Joseph H. Parks, *General Edmund Kirby Smith, CSA* (Baton Rouge: Louisiana State University Press, 1982), 195; Smith is also quoted in Joseph H. Parks, *General Leonidas Polk, CSA* (Baton Rouge: Louisiana State University Press, 1965), 249.

8. Connelly, *Army of the Heartland*, 205; McWhiney, "Controversy in Kentucky," 11; Parks, *General Edmund Kirby Smith*, 201–2; Noe, *Perryville*, 31–32; Grady McWhiney, *Braxton Bragg and Confederate Defeat* (Tuscaloosa: University of Alabama Press, 1969), 272; Parks, *General Leonidas Polk*, 250–51.

9. *OR*, vol. 16, pt. 2, 733–34, 753; Morgan is also quoted in James A. Ramage, *Rebel Raider: The Life of General John Hunt Morgan* (Lexington: University Press of Kentucky, 1886), 101–2; Noe, *Perryville*, 31.

10. "Bold move" quoted in McDonough, *War in Kentucky*, 81; Connolly, *Heartland*, 211–12, 216; Noe, *Perryville*, 39–40.

11. James R. Fleming, *Band of Brothers: Company C, 9th Tennessee Infantry* (Shippensburg, PA: White Mane Publishing Company, 1996), 30; Losson, *Tennessee's Forgotten Warriors*, 61.

12. John Cavanaugh, *Historical Sketch of Obion Avalanche, Company H, Ninth Tennessee Infantry, Confederate States of America* (Union City, TN: Commercial Printery, 1922), 196.

13. George D. Ewing, "General Bragg's Kentucky Campaign," *Confederate Veteran* 34 (June 1926): 215; Hall quoted in Losson, *Tennessee's Forgotten Warriors*, 64.

14. For correspondence between Bragg and Smith, see *OR*, vol. 16, pt. 2, 749, 759, 775; Buell moves from Nashville, *OR*, vol. 16, pt. 1, 1,023;

Stephen D. Engle, "Success, Failure, and the Guillotine: Don Carlos Buell and the Campaign for the Bluegrass State," *Register of the Kentucky Historical Society* 96 (Autumn 1998): 320–21.

Chapter 2

15. *OR*, vol. 16, pt. 1, 1,023–24; Noe, *Perryville*, 95–96, 98; Engle, *Don Carlos Buell*, 303–4; Daniel, *Days of Glory*, 141.
16. *OR*, vol. 16, pt. 2, 900–2; Connelly, *Army of the Heartland*, 235.
17. *OR*, vol. 16, pt. 1, 1,019; Kurt Holman, Perryville Casualty Computer Database File, Perryville Battlefield State Historic Site, Perryville, Kentucky (hereafter cited as Holman, Casualties).
18. Noe, *Perryville*, 110; *OR*, vol. 16, pt. 1, 1,120.
19. B.F. Cheatham, "The Battle of Perryville," *Southern Bivouac* 4 (April 1886): 704; Kenneth A. Hafendorfer, *Perryville: Battle for Kentucky* (Louisville: KH Press, 1991), 128–29; Marcus B. Toney, *The Privations of a Private* (Nashville, TN, 1905), 42.
20. Watkins, *"Co. Aytch,"* 81, W.T. Dixon III, ed., "A Chapter from the Civil War Travels of William A. Brown," unpublished manuscript in the files of the Perryville Battlefield Preservation Association, Perryville, Kentucky.
21. *OR*, vol. 16, pt. 1, 1,110, 1,101–2; Connelly, *Army of the Heartland*, 259–60. For information on the fight at Peter's Hill, see Noe, *Perryville*, 145–56; McDonough, *War in Kentucky*, 220–23.
22. McWhiney, *Braxton Bragg and Confederate Defeat*, 314; McWhiney, "Controversy in Kentucky," 32; Stanley F. Horn, *The Army of Tennessee* (Wilmington, NC: Broadfoot Publishing Company, 1987), 183; Connelly, *Army of the Heartland*, 262; Cheatham, "Battle of Perryville," 704; Buell obituary, *Confederate Veteran*, 536; Noe, *Perryville*, 170–71.
23. *OR*, vol. 16, pt. 1, 1,119; Noe, *Perryville*, 171–72; Robert S. Cameron, *Staff Ride Handbook for the Battle of Perryville, 8 October 1862* (Fort Leavenworth, KS: Combat Studies Institute Press, 2005), 164.

Chapter 3

24. Brigadier General George E. Maney, "Report of the Action Near Perryville, KY, Oct. 8th, 1862," October 29, 1862, Braxton Bragg Papers, Western Reserve Historical Society (hereafter cited as Maney's report); Brigadier General Daniel S. Donelson, "Report of the Part Taken in the Battle of Perryville by the 1st Brigade, 1st Div., Rt. Wg., Army of the Miss.," October 27, 1862, William P. Palmer Collection of Civil War Manuscripts, Western Reserve Historical Society (hereafter cited as Donelson's report); Hafendorfer, *Perryville*, 167.

25. Marshall P. Thatcher, *A Hundred Battles in the West: The Second Michigan Cavalry* (Detroit, 1884), 79; Loomis is also quoted in Hafendorfer, *Perryville*, 167; and Daniel, *Days of Glory*, 148.

26. Davis Biggs, "Incidents in Battle of Perryville, KY," *Confederate Veteran* 33 (April 1925): 141; Connelly, *Army of the Heartland*, 263.

27. John Beatty, *The Citizen-Soldier: The Memoirs of a Civil War Volunteer* (Lincoln: University of Nebraska Press, 1998; originally published 1879), 178; *Cincinnati Daily Enquirer*, October 14, 1862; Noe, *Perryville*, 177–78; William A. Brown, quoted from http://www.geocities.com/Heartland/6519/travch08.html; Cameron, *Staff Ride Handbook*, 165; Prokopowicz, *All for the Regiment*, 165.

28. "Dear Amanda" letter, October 12, 1862, George W. Landrum Letters, Ohio Historical Society, Columbus.

29. Frank Moore, ed., *The Rebellion Record: A Diary of American Events* (New York: Arno Press, 1977; originally published 1861–68), 5:529.

30. Thomas H. Malone, *Memoir of Thomas H. Malone* (Nashville, TN, 1928), 128.

31. Biggs, "Incidents in Battle of Perryville," 141; Dixon, "Chapter from the Civil War Travels."

32. *OR*, vol. 16, pt. 1, 1,116, 1,118.

33. Pickett, "Reminiscences of Murfreesoboro," 450.

34. "Dear Amanda" letter, October 12, 1862, Landrum Letters, Ohio Historical Society.

35. Donelson's report; Captain W.W. Carnes, "Artillery at the Battle of Perryville," *Confederate Veteran* 33 (January 1925): 8; Hafendorfer, *Perryville*, 198.

36. Noe, *Perryville*, 183; McDonough, *War in Kentucky*, 241. Perryville park manager Kurt Holman noted that archaeological evidence—fired ten-pounder Schenkl shells—found in the area where Wharton operated

points to Bush's Battery also firing at Wharton's horsemen. E-mail correspondence with Holman, December 30, 2013.

37. *OR*, vol. 16, pt. 1, 1,045, 1,049; Noe, *Perryville*, 186; "Dear Amanda" letter, October 12, 1862, Landrum Letters, Ohio Historical Society; *New Albany Daily Ledger*, "Battle of Chaplin Hill," October 16, 1862; Henry Fales Perry, *History of the Thirty-Eighth Regiment Indiana Volunteer Infantry* (Palo Alto, CA: F.A. Stuart, 1906), 29; B.F. Scribner, *How Soldiers Were Made* (New Albany, IN, 1887), 58. McCook had sent the 33rd Ohio "into the woods on the right as skirmishers to ascertain if any enemy was present in that vicinity." *OR*, vol. 16, pt. 1, 1,039.

38. E.W. Gilbert, "What Battery Was It?" *National Tribune* 25 (May 16, 1907): 6.

39. McDonough, *War in Kentucky*, 241; Kenneth A. Hafendorfer, *They Died by Twos and Tens: The Confederate Cavalry in the Kentucky Campaign of 1862* (Louisville: KH Press, 1995), 720–21; John M. Claiborne, "Several Errors Corrected," *Confederate Veteran* 6 (August 1898): 375; Angus L. Waddle, *Three Years with the Armies of the Ohio and the Cumberland* (Chillicothe, OH: Scioto Gazette Book and Job Office, 1889), 30.

40. Maney's report; Donelson's report; Brigadier General A.P. Stewart, "Report of Action near Perryville, Ky., Oct. 8, 1862," Braxton Bragg Papers, Western Reserve Historical Society (hereafter cited as Stewart's report); McWhiney, "Controversy in Kentucky," 33. James R. Thompson of the 16th Tennessee wrote, "We had to climb a hill which was difficult to ascend." James R. Thompson, "Hear the Wax Fry: Memoirs of the War Between the States," transcript in 16th Tennessee Infantry File, Perryville Battlefield State Historic Site, Perryville, Kentucky, 9. Savage wrote that the bluffs were "steep and difficult to get up." John H. Savage, *The Life of John H. Savage: Citizen, Soldier, Lawyer, Congressman* (Nashville, TN, 1905), transcript in 16th Tennessee Infantry File, Perryville Battlefield State Historic Site, Perryville, Kentucky.

41. E-mail correspondence with Kurt Holman, manager, Perryville Battlefield State Historic Site, December 29, 2013. Because Simonson's Battery was actively engaged in the artillery duel, this would have been the battery that Donelson noted was engaged in "a constant firing." In addition, in examining the terrain of the battlefield, Simonson's Battery would have been visible to Donelson's men, who formed in the area above Walker's Bend that is now near the entrance to the Perryville Battlefield State Historic Site. Other batteries would not have been visible, and they would not have been firing. Simonson's Battery was, however, actively engaged.

42. Quoted in McDonough, *War in Kentucky*, 243–44, and Hafendorfer, *Perryville*, 199. While several sources attribute the anecdote as occurring at Perryville, Private Sam Watkins of the 1st Tennessee reported that this episode instead occurred at the Battle of Chickamauga. As Cheatham was known to speak with a profane tongue on more than one occasion, one wonders if this episode happened more than once. Watkins, *"Co. Aytch,"* 118.

43. Thompson, "Hear the Wax Fry"; Thomas R. Hooper, "Diary from May 19–December 28, 1862," transcript in 16th Tennessee Infantry File, Perryville Battlefield State Historic Site; Johnston quoted in McWhiney, *Braxton Bragg and Confederate Defeat*, 316.

44. Waddle, *Three Years with the Armies*, 30; Landrum quoted in McDonough, *War in Kentucky*, 243; *OR*, vol. 16, pt. 1, 1,040; Noe, *Perryville*, 197.

45. Hafendorfer, *Perryville*, 205; McDonough, *War in Kentucky*, 245–46; *OR*, vol. 16, pt. 1, 1,111.

46. For Tyler, see Stuart W. Sanders, "One Last Gallant Defense," *MHQ: The Quarterly Journal of Military History* (Spring 2006): 44–51. Savage's memoir, written in the third person, blames Donelson and Cheatham for Savage's large losses and accuses these two generals of intentionally deploying him alone in order to have him killed. Savage also claimed that Cheatham and Donelson were drunk during the fight and that both had "no great knowledge or ability" and were "without military instinct and with but little knowledge of the art of war." Savage, *Life of John H. Savage*.

47. Donelson's report; Savage, *Life of John H. Savage*, 120. T.A. Head of the 16th Tennessee wrote that "[t]he brigade was subjected to a fearful cross-fire, both of infantry and artillery." T.A. Head, "A Most Remarkable Wound...," *Confederate Veteran* 5 (August 1897): 435. James R. Thompson recalled that Savage was riding at the head of his men when his horse was struck. Thompson, "Hear the Wax Fry," 9.

48. Donelson report; Walling quoted in Savage, *Life of John H. Savage*, 126.

49. Clark quoted in McDonough, *War in Kentucky*, 248; Thomas A. Head, *Campaigns and Battles of the Sixteenth Regiment, Tennessee Volunteers* (Nashville, TN: Cumberland Presbyterian Publishing House, 1885), 95–96.

50. *Confederate Veteran* 7, "Col. John Savage..." (March 1899): 118; Biggs, "Incidents in Battle of Perryville," 142.

51. A.J. Cantrell, "Vivid Experiences in Prison," *Confederate Veteran* 16 (May 1908): 216; *Confederate Veteran* 22, "The Cantrells of Tennessee" (October 1914): 476; Holman, Casualties; Noe, *Perryville*, 369.

52. Head, "Most Remarkable Wound," 435; McDonough, *War in Kentucky*, 248.

53. Walling quoted in Savage, *Life of John H. Savage*; Noe, *Perryville*, 202; *OR*, vol. 16, pt. 1, 1,053, 1,049; Whitelaw Reid, *Ohio in the War: Her Statesmen, Her Generals, and Soldiers* (Cincinnati, OH: Moore, Wilstack, and Baldwin, 1868), 2:219.

54. Biggs, "Incidents in Battle of Perryville," 141.

55. Savage, *Life of John H. Savage*, 115; Donelson's report; Noe, *Perryville*, 202; Head, *Campaigns and Battles of the Sixteenth Regiment*, 96; Thompson, "Hear the Wax Fry," 10.

56. Alf Burnett, *Humorous, Pathetic, and Descriptive Incidents of the War* (Cincinnati, OH: R.W. Carroll and Company, 1864), 18–20.

Chapter 4

57. Watkins, *"Co. Aytch,"* 81.

58. Jon L. Wakelyn, ed., *Biographical Dictionary of the Confederacy* (Westport, CT: Greenwood Press, 1977), 308; Losson, *Tennessee's Forgotten Warriors*, 48; Mark M. Boatner III, *The Civil War Dictionary* (New York: Vintage Books, 1991), 507; Patricia L. Faust, ed., *Historical Times Illustrated Encyclopedia of the Civil War* (New York: HarperPerennial, 1986), 472.

59. Wakelyn, *Biographical Dictionary of the Confederacy*, 308; Faust, *Historical Times Illustrated Encyclopedia*, 472; Boatner, *Civil War Dictionary*, 507; Prentice quoted in "J. Tom Brown," *Confederate Veteran* 15 (June 1907): 273.

60. Kurt Holman, ed., Perryville Regimental Computer Database File, Perryville Battlefield State Historic Site, Perryville, Kentucky (hereafter cited as Holman, Regiments).

61. W.M. Pollard, "Brief History of the First Tennessee," *Confederate Veteran* 17 (1909): 543; *Confederate Veteran* 19, "Lieut. Charles H. King" (March 1911): 130; Holman, Regiments.

62. *Confederate Veteran* 13, "Captain Henry Hunter Smith" (May 1905): 236; Faust, *Historical Times Illustrated Encyclopedia*, 472; Boatner, *Civil War Dictionary*, 507; Connelly, *Civil War Tennessee*, 47; Maney and Cheatham quoted in Losson, *Tennessee's Forgotten Warriors*, 48–49; Larry J. Daniel, *Shiloh: The Battle that Changed the Civil War* (New York: Simon and Schuster, 1997), 219; "piles of mangled bodies" quoted from Daniel, *Shiloh*, 247; Pollard, "Brief History of the First Tennessee," 543.

63. *Confederate Veteran* 22, "James Martin Cartmell" (March 1914): 136; 6th Tennessee statistics from Losson, *Tennessee's Forgotten Warriors*, 47;

Cavanaugh, *Historical Sketch of Obion Avalanche*, 171; Holman, Regiments; Fleming, *Band of Brothers*, 28.

64. Holman, Regiments.
65. Ibid.; Noe, *Perryville*, 381.
66. Holman, Regiments; Noe, *Perryville*, 369–70. For a biographical treatment of Cheatham, see Losson, *Tennessee's Forgotten Warriors*. For a biographical treatment of Stewart, see Sam Davis Elliott, *Soldier of Tennessee* (Baton Rouge: Louisiana State University Press, 1999).
67. Losson, *Tennessee's Forgotten Warriors*, 48; Connelly, *Army of the Heartland*, 223; McWhiney, *Braxton Bragg and Confederate Defeat*, 262, 276–77.
68. *OR*, vol. 16, pt. 1, 1,118.
69. Maney's report. Maney noted that the "irregularity of the ground" made it impossible to advance up the bluffs in a line of battle. Another Confederate officer recalled that the bluffs over the river were "rocky and precipitous" and proved to be an "impossible ascent." *OR*, vol. 16, pt. 1, 1,115. Cheatham wrote, "I in person moved Maney's brigade by the right flank several hundred yards." Cheatham, "Battle of Perryville," 705.
70. Maney's report; McDonough, *War in Kentucky*, 248–49; Noe, *Perryville*, 204.
71. *OR*, vol. 16, pt. 1, 1,115.
72. Maney's report.
73. Ibid.
74. Ibid.
75. Carroll, *Autobiography and Reminiscences*, 23–24; Losson, *Tennessee's Forgotten Warriors*, 67; McDonough, *War in Kentucky*, 249.
76. Maney's report.
77. Ibid.; *OR*, vol. 16, pt. 1, 1,113–14; McDonough, *War in Kentucky*, 249; Hafendorfer, *Perryville*, 215; Curtwright quoted in A.J. West, "The Great Battle of Perryville, Ky.," unidentified newspaper (possibly the *Atlanta Reporter*), October 1892, photocopy in 41st Georgia Infantry File, Perryville Battlefield State Historic Site, Perryville, Kentucky; Stuart W. Sanders, "All Did Their Duty Nobly Well," *America's Civil War* (November 2004): 24. The 6th Tennessee had 314 soldiers, the 9th Tennessee had 378 and the 41st Georgia had 520. The 1st Tennessee contained 400 soldiers, and the 27th Tennessee had 210. Noe, *Perryville*, 370.

Chapter 5

78. Samuel M. Starling, "Dearest Daughters" letter, November 16, 1862, Lewis-Starling Manuscript Collection, Western Kentucky University.

79. *OR*, vol. 16, pt. 1, 294; McDonough, *War in Kentucky*, 249; Hafendorfer, *Perryville*, 216. The *Cincinnati Daily Enquirer* reported, "This strip of timber formed a covered way by which the rebels stealthily advanced until they were near our lines, when, suddenly, deploying to the left, they occupied the whole space in front of Jackson's division, and rushed upon it with demoniac yells." *Cincinnati Daily Enquirer*, October 14, 1862.

80. Moore, *Rebellion Record*, 5:515; *OR*, vol. 16, pt. 1, 1,060, 1,118; McDonough, *War in Kentucky*, 250; Maney's report; Hafendorfer, *Perryville*, 239.

81. *OR*, vol. 16, pt. 1, 1,115.

82. Ibid., 1,059, 1,062; Moore, *Rebellion Record*, 5:514.

83. *OR*, vol. 16, pt. 1, 1,063; Hafendorfer, *Perryville*, 199; Moore, *Rebellion Record*, 5:514; Holman, Regiments; Noe, *Perryville*, 383; Reverend J.N. Fradenburgh, *In Memoriam: Henry Harrison Cumings, Charlotte J. Cumings* (Oil City, PA: Derrick Publishing Company, 1913), 44.

84. J. Montgomery Wright, "Notes of a Staff-Officer at Perryville," *Battles and Leaders of the Civil War* (reprint, Secaucus, NJ: Castle Books, n.d.), 3:61.

85. *OR*, vol. 16, pt. 1, 1,060, 1,113; Moore, *Rebellion Record*, 5:514; Sanders, "All Did Their Duty," 25.

86. Maney's report.

87. Thomas T. Haver, ed., *Forty-Eight Days: The 105th Ohio Volunteer Infantry, Camp Cleveland, Ohio, to Perryville, Kentucky* (Amherst, MA: Collective Copies, 1997), 35–36.

88. *OR*, vol. 16, pt. 1, 1,062–63; Frederick H. Dyer, *A Compendium of the War of the Rebellion* (New York: Thomas Yoseloff, 1959), 3:1,098; Holman, Regiments; Moore, *Rebellion Record*, 5:514.

89. Moore, *Rebellion Record*, 5:514; *OR*, vol. 16, pt. 1, 1,060; McDonough, *War in Kentucky*, 253; Hafendorfer, *Perryville*, 216.

90. A.D. Cleaver, "Dear Wife and Children," undated letter in the 123rd Illinois Infantry File, Perryville Battlefield State Historic Site, Perryville, Kentucky; Paul M. Angle, ed., *Three Years in the Army of the Cumberland: The Letters and Diary of Major James A. Connolly* (Bloomington: Indiana University Press, 1959), 21.

91. Cleaver letter; Hafendorfer, *Perryville*, 216; Holman, Regiments.

92. *New York Times*, October 11, 1862; McDonough, *War in Kentucky*, 253; Boatner, *Civil War Dictionary*, 431; William Henry Perrin, ed., *County of Christian, Kentucky* (Chicago: F.A. Battey Publishing Company, 1881), 188–89; Thomas Speed, *The Union Regiments of Kentucky* (Louisville, KY: Courier-Journal Job Printing Company, 1897), 63, 133–34. The *Louisville Journal* called Jackson "every inch a patriot, a soldier, and a man." *Louisville Journal*, October 11, 1862. For Jackson's Mexican-American War duel against Thomas F. Marshall, see Cassius Marcellus Clay, *The Life of Cassius Marcellus Clay* (Cincinnati, OH: J. Fletcher Brennan and Company, 1886) 2:140–41; J. Winston Coleman Jr., *Famous Kentucky Duels* (Lexington, KY: Henry Clay Press, 1969), 143–44.

93. Charles C. Gilbert, "On the Field of Perryville," *Battles and Leaders of the Civil War*, 3:57n. See also Stuart W. Sanders, "3 Top Union Officers Lost in Battle of Perryville," *Washington Times* (January 22, 2000): B3.

94. Starling letter, Western Kentucky University; *OR*, vol. 16, pt. 1, 1,060.

95. Richard G. Stone, *Kentucky's Fighting Men* (Lexington: University Press of Kentucky, 1982), 16.

96. Starling letter, Western Kentucky University. There were several different accounts of Jackson's death. Major James Connolly of the 123rd Illinois stated that he was standing a few feet from Jackson when the general was killed. "He was on foot," Connolly wrote, "and had just advised me to dismount when he fell." A *New York Times* correspondent noted that "Jackson deliberately lighted a cigar; just as he had lighted it, a ball from the enemy struck him, killing him instantly." Angle, *Three Years in the Army*, 21; *Times* correspondent quoted in *Harper's Weekly*, November 1, 1862. Another source wrongly stated that Jackson was struck in the right side of his chest by a shell fragment, yelled, "Oh God!" and fell from his horse and died. Samuel P. Bates, *History of Pennsylvania Volunteers, 1861–5* (Harrisburg, PA: B. Singerly, 1869), 2:1,078n. A Louisville paper reported that Jackson was killed while "in the act of rallying his men." *Louisville Journal*, October 10, 1862.

97. Starling letter, Western Kentucky University.

98. *OR*, vol. 16, pt. 1, 296.

99. Ibid., 1,115, 1,113; West, "Great Battle of Perryville"; Sanders, "All Did Their Duty," 25.

100. Maney mistakenly believed that the large regiments facing him, the 123rd Illinois and the 105th Ohio, were an entire brigade. Maney's report. Captain Starling stated that the rail fence was 130 yards away from Parsons' Battery. Starling letter, Western Kentucky University.

Chapter 6

101. Fleming, *Band of Brothers*, 33.

102. Ibid.

103. *OR*, vol. 16, pt. 1, 1,118.

104. Ibid., 1,064; Hafendorfer, *Perryville*, 216; Haver, *Forty-Eight Days*, 36; Dyer, *Compendium of the War*, 3:1,542; McDonough, *War in Kentucky*, 253; Moore, *Rebellion Record*, 5:514; Holman, Regiments.

105. James Glauser, ed., *The Civil War Diary of Private Josiah Ayre*, photocopy in 105th Ohio Infantry Regiment File, Perryville Battlefield State Historic Site, Perryville, Kentucky, 19; McDonough, *War in Kentucky*, 301.

106. Haver, *Forty-Eight Days*, 35; Lester Dewitt Taylor Diary, U.S. Army Military History Institute, Civil War Miscellaneous Collection, Carlisle Barracks, Pennsylvania; Charles K. Radcliffe, "Terrill's Brigade at Perryville," *National Tribune* 24 (June 14, 1906): 3. Cumings of Parsons' Battery wrote, "It was the hottest fire I ever experienced as you may well know when I state that we were under fire only about twenty minutes and in that time two-thirds of all the men of our battery on the field were killed or wounded. The battery was disbanded and I returned to my regiment." Fradenburgh, *In Memoriam*, 47.

107. Haver, *Forty-Eight Days*, 35, 37. Cumings of Parsons' Battery called Terrill the "patron" of the unit. Frandenburgh, *In Memoriam*, 47.

108. Bliss Morse of the 105th Ohio stated that "the right wing of our regiment [was] where the left should have been." Haver, *Forty-Eight Days*, 35–36; Glauser, *Civil War Diary of Private Josiah Ayre*, 20.

109. Haver, *Forty-Eight Days*, 36, 39; Glauser, *Civil War Diary of Private Josiah Ayre*, 20. Lester Taylor of the 105th Ohio wrote that as the Buckeyes got on their knees and returned fire, so many of "the balls passed over us." He added that "I never knew hail to fall faster than the bullets did." Taylor Diary, U.S. Army Military History Institute.

110. McDonough, *War in Kentucky*, 301–2.

111. Maney's report; W.H. Smith, "Melanchthon Smith's Battery," *Confederate Veteran* 12 (November 1904): 532; Holman, Regiments.

112. Malone, *Memoir of Thomas H. Malone*, 129.

113. Smith, "Melanchthon Smith's Battery," 532; Larry J. Daniel, *Cannoneers in Gray: The Field Artillery of the Army of Tennessee, 1861–1865* (Tuscaloosa: University of Alabama Press, 1984), 50–51.

114. Smith, "Melanchthon Smith's Battery," 532.

115. Kurt Holman, Battle of Perryville Timeline, Perryville Battlefield State Historic Site, Perryville, Kentucky; Hafendorfer, *Perryville*, 240; Hambleton Tapp, ed., "The Battle of Perryville, October 8, 1862, As Described in the Diary of Captain Robert B. Taylor," *Register of the Kentucky Historical Society* 60 (1962): 275; Moore, *Rebellion Record*, 5:514; Holman, Regiments.

116. Holman, Regiments; Dyer, *Compendium of the War*, 3:1,080; Illinois native quoted in McDonough, *War in Kentucky*, 253.

117. Holman, Regiments; *OR*, vol. 16, pt. 1, 1,062; Nicky Hughes, "Theophilus Toulmin Garrard," *Kentucky Encyclopedia* (Lexington: University Press of Kentucky, 1992), 364; Federal officer quoted in John Coburn, "A General Recalls Civil War Experiences in Kentucky During 1861–1862," *Kentucky Explorer* (June 1997): 49.

118. Holman, Regiments.

119. Ibid.

120. *OR*, vol. 16, pt. 1, 1,063; Hafendorfer, *Perryville*, 240.

121. Malone, *Memoir of Thomas H. Malone*, 129; Maney's report.

122. Malone, *Memoir of Thomas H. Malone*, 130; Maney's report; McDonough, *War in Kentucky*, 251; *OR*, vol. 16, pt. 1, 1,115.

123. *OR*, vol. 16, pt. 1, 1,113; Sanders, "All Did Their Duty," 25. Maney began his trek down the line from the right, where the 41st Georgia was positioned. It is probable that he was with the 41st Georgia when the brigade initially became pinned down. It was a new regiment, and he may have had more confidence in his veteran Tennesseans. Thus, he chose to be near the green Georgians.

124. *OR*, vol. 16, pt. 1, 1,118; Bianca Morse Federico, ed., "The Letters of John Holbrook Morse, 1861–1865," photocopy of manuscript in 105th Ohio Infantry File, Perryville Battlefield State Historic Site, Perryville, Kentucky, 63; Haver, *Forty-Eight Days*, 36.

125. West, "Great Battle of Perryville."

126. Federico, "Letters of John Holbrook Morse," 63; *OR*, vol. 16, pt. 1, 1,065; Glauser, *Civil War Diary of Private Josiah Ayre*, 20. Maney believed that the accuracy of Turner's battery contributed to the Confederates' success. He wrote that when the Northerners were "[t]orn in flank by our shot and shell and pressed with a desperate and reckless courage on the part of the entire line," the Southern momentum improved. Maney's report.

127. Maney's report; Carroll, *Autobiography and Reminiscences*, 24; *OR*, vol. 16, pt. 1, 1,115.

128. Cheatham, "Battle of Perryville," 705.

129. Malone, *Memoir of Thomas H. Malone*, 133. Cheatham also found Jackson's corpse. He wrote that "a few minutes" after Maney's command moved away from the fence, "I found the dead body of General Jackson, whom I had known well for years." Cheatham, "Battle of Perryville," 705.

130. Maney's report; Hafendorfer, *Perryville*, 239.

131. Malone, *Memoir of Thomas H. Malone*, 131.

Chapter 7

132. Hafendorfer, *Perryville*, 240; McDonough, *War in Kentucky*, 250. Perryville park manager Kurt Holman believes that the gap that opened up between the 6th Tennessee and 41st Georgia "would have been approximately the same as Parsons' frontage." Therefore, the gap was caused because the Confederate troops instinctively avoided moving "directly into the muzzles of the cannon." Once Parsons' gunners ran away, the 27th Tennessee moved into this gap. E-mail correspondence with Holman, December 29, 2013.

133. Fleming, *Band of Brothers*, 33; *OR*, vol. 16, pt. 1, 1,116, 1,115.

134. Quoted in McDonough, *War in Kentucky*, 251; Tapp, "Battle of Perryville," 275.

135. Maney's report.

136. Ibid.; kicked by the horse from Seth Warner, "George Earl Maney: Soldier, Railroader, and Diplomat," *Tennessee Historical Quarterly* 65 (Summer 2006): 133.

137. Maney's report; Cheatham, "Battle of Perryville," 705.

138. Maney's report.

139. Charles W. Miles, "Col. Hume R. Feild," *Confederate Veteran* 29 (September 1921): 325.

140. Maney's report.

141. Ibid.

142. Maney's report; Hafendorfer, *Perryville*, 242.

143. Cheatham, "Battle of Perryville," 705; *OR*, vol. 16, pt. 1, 1,156–57; Hafendorfer, *Perryville*, 242.

144. Malone, *Memoir of Thomas H. Malone*, 135.

145. Ibid., 130; Radcliffe, "Terrill's Brigade at Perryville," 3; *OR*, vol. 16, pt. 1, 1,115; Porter also quoted in Losson, *Tennessee's Forgotten Warriors*, 69.

146. *OR*, vol. 16, pt. 1, 1,157; Malone, *Memoir of Thomas H. Malone*, 131.

147. Wright, "Notes of a Staff-Officer," 3:61; *OR*, vol. 16, pt. 1, 1,063–64, 1,041; Horn, *Army of Tennessee*, 454–55; Noe, *Perryville*, 211. All of Parsons' guns were captured except for one twelve-pounder field howitzer. Holman, Regiments. This was easily done, a correspondent noted, since the "rebel sharpshooters and skirmishers shot down the horses of Capt. Parsons' battery." *Louisville Journal*, October 14, 1862.

148. Smith, "Melanchthon Smith's Battery," 532; *Harper's Weekly* (November 1, 1862): 695.

149. Cavanaugh, *Historical Sketch of Obion Avalanche*, 179, 219.

150. Holman, Regiments; *OR*, vol. 16, pt. 1, 1,061.

151. Maney's report; *OR*, vol. 16, pt. 1, 1,118.

152. *OR*, vol. 16, pt. 1, 1,117, 1,113; Fleming, *Band of Brothers*, 34.

153. Tapp, "Battle of Perryville," 275–76; Hafendorfer, *Perryville*, 241–43; Stewart's report.

154. Hafendorfer, *Perryville*, 243; Federico, "Letters of John Holbrook Morse," 63–64.

155. *OR*, vol. 16, pt. 1, 1,065; Haver, *Forty-Eight Days*, 36.

156. Glauser, *Civil War Diary of Private Josiah Ayre*, 20–22.

157. Haver, *Forty-Eight Days*, 37.

158. Maney's report.

Chapter 8

159. Ibid.

160. Michael H. Fitch, *Echoes of the Civil War as I Hear Them* (New York: R.F. Fenno and Company, 1905), 54, 64; Leo M. Kaiser, ed., "Civil War Letters of Charles W. Carr of the 21st Wisconsin Volunteers," *Wisconsin Magazine of History* 43 (Summer 1960): 265; Stuart W. Sanders, "Perryville's Bloody Cornfield," *America's Civil War* (September 2002): 32.

161. Holman, Regiments; Kaiser, "Civil War Letters of Charles W. Carr," 268–69; Fitch, *Echoes of the Civil War*, 61–62; Sanders, "Perryville's Bloody Cornfield," 32. The 21st Wisconsin was organized at Oshkosh, Wisconsin, and was mustered into service on September 5, 1862. Dyer, *Compendium of the War*, 3:1,682.

162. John Henry Otto, "War Memories," transcript of memoirs in 21st Wisconsin Infantry File, Perryville Battlefield State Historic Site, Perryville, Kentucky.

163. Ibid., 90–91; Fitch, *Echoes of the Civil War*, 59.

164. Fitch, *Echoes of the Civil War*, 60; Sanders, "Perryville's Bloody Cornfield," 34.

165. Fitch, *Echoes of the Civil War*, 60; Sanders, "Perryville's Bloody Cornfield," 34.

166. Fitch, *Echoes of the Civil War*, 60.

167. Otto, "War Memories," 91.

168. Ibid., 91–92; Fitch, *Echoes of the Civil War*, 74.

169. Otto, "War Memories," 92, 102; *OR*, vol. 16, pt. 1, 1,156; John C. Starkweather, "Perryville: Letter from Gen. Starkweather, and His Official Report," *National Tribune* 6 (November 4, 1886): 2.

170. *OR*, vol. 16, pt. 1, 1,113; Malone, *Memoir of Thomas H. Malone*, 130; Holman, Regiments; Hafendorfer, *Perryville*, 267; Sanders, "All Did Their Duty," 73; Maney's report. Although some sources state that McDaniel died on October 31, his death was mentioned in a letter from Benjamin Mills to Maria Evans on October 21. Maria Evans Claiborne, "A Woman's Memories of the Sixties," *Confederate Veteran* 13 (February 1905): 64.

171. Fitch, *Echoes of the Civil War*, 74, 60–61; Otto, "War Memories," 92.

172. Otto, "War Memories," 92–93.

173. Edward Ferguson, "The Army of the Cumberland Under Buell," speech delivered December 5, 1888, photocopy in the 1st Wisconsin Infantry Regiment File, Perryville Battlefield State Historic Site, Perryville, Kentucky, 429.

174. *OR*, vol. 16, pt. 1, 1,116; Hafendorfer, *Perryville*, 267.

175. Fitch, *Echoes of the Civil War*, 61; Otto, "War Memories," 93.

176. Otto, "War Memories," 95.

177. Holman, Regiments; Holman, Casualties; Elias H. Hoover, "Battle of Perryville," *National Tribune* 8 (June 20, 1889): 3; Otto, "War Memories," 92.

178. Fitch, *Echoes of the Civil War*, 64. Thus, Fitch blamed Rousseau, his division commander, and Starkweather, the brigade commander, for placing the 21st in a precarious position. Terrill is also to blame for not extricating the 21st Wisconsin when he had the chance. Instead of directing the new troops to attempt a bayonet charge, Terrill should have realized that the outnumbered regiment would be crushed by Maney's Brigade. Terrill, however, heartbroken over the loss of his battery, was not interested in extricating infantry from another brigade.

Chapter 9

179. McDonough, *War in Kentucky*, 273; Rousseau on Starkweather in *OR*, vol. 16, pt. 1, 1,045.

180. McDonough, *War in Kentucky*, 273; Holman, Casualties; Dyer, *Compendium of the War*, 3:1,112.

181. Holman, Regiments; *Louisville Journal*, October 13, 1862; Dyer, *Compendium of the War*, 3:1,196; "great haste" from *Valparaiso Republic*, November 13, 1862.

182. Holman, Regiments; Dyer, *Compendium of the War*, 3:1,673; Ferguson, "Army of the Cumberland Under Buell," 426.

183. Holman, Regiments; Bates, *History of Pennsylvania Volunteers*, 2:1,077; Harrison C. Williams, "Regimental History of the 79th Pennsylvania Volunteers of the Civil War: The Lancaster County Regiment," *Journal of the Lancaster County Historical Society* 84 (1980): 17.

184. McDonough, *War in Kentucky*, 273; Boatner, *Civil War Dictionary*, 793; Daniel, *Days of Glory*, 150; Beatty, *Citizen-Soldier*, 270, 280; Hoover, "Battle of Perryville," 3.

185. John Fitch, *Annals of the Army of the Cumberland* (Philadelphia: J.P. Lippincott and Company, 1864), 80–85; Coburn, "General Recalls Civil War Experiences," 49; Noe, *Perryville*, 95–96; Daniel, *Days of Glory*, 6–7; Prokopowicz, *All for the Regiment*, 12–13.

186. Ferguson, "Army of the Cumberland Under Buell," 429; *Louisville Journal*, October 14, 1862. A Union soldier in the 33rd Ohio wrote, "The splendid figure of General Rousseau on his thoroughbred Kentucky horse was always in our front and where the fight was hottest there he was to be seen cheering and encouraging his men." Waddle, *Three Years with the Armies*, 30. Hoover of the 1st Wisconsin said that Starkweather also rode his horse across the field, spinning his hat on his sword. Hoover, "Battle of Perryville," 3. See also Daniel, *Days of Glory*, 151, and Noe, *Perryville*, 244–45.

187. Starling quoted in Stone, *Kentucky's Fighting Men*, 18.

188. *National Tribune* 2, "Soldiers' Anecdotes" (March 1879): 19.

189. Tapp, "Battle of Perryville," 277.

190. *OR*, vol. 16, pt. 1, 1,115; Malone, *Memoir of Thomas H. Malone*, 131–32; Cheatham, "Battle of Perryville," 705.

191. Feild reported the regiment "was ordered immediately forward to take another battery about a half mile in advance, planted on a very steep hill,

commanding a large corn field through which we had to advance." *OR*, vol. 16, pt. 1, 1,113–14; Miles, "Col. Hume R. Feild," 325.

192. Maney's report; *OR*, vol. 16, pt. 1, 1,114; *Valparaiso Republic*, November 13, 1862.

193. Hafendorfer, *Perryville*, 268; *OR*, vol. 16, pt. 1, 1,117–118.

194. Ferguson, "Army of the Cumberland Under Buell," 430; *Louisville Journal*, October 14, 1862.

195. Otto, "War Memories," 93–94; also quoted in Noe, *Perryville*, 253.

196. Holman, Regiments; William Mitchell, "My Dear Father" letter, October 9, 1862, transcript in 1st Wisconsin Infantry Regiment File, Perryville Battlefield State Historic Site, Perryville, Kentucky.

197. Watkins, *"Co. Aytch,"* 82.

198. Ibid., 84; John A. Bruce, "Battle of Perryville, Ky., As Told in an Old Letter by J.A. Bruce," *Confederate Veteran* 10 (1902): 177.

199. Maney's report; Toney, *Privations of a Private*, 43–44; Watkins, *"Co. Aytch,"* 83. Maney, in his after-action report, noted that Patterson was killed during the first charge up Starkweather's hill.

200. Watkins, *"Co. Aytch,"* 83.

201. Mitchell, "My Dear Father" letter; Holman, Regiments.

202. *OR*, vol. 16, pt. 1, 1,116; Carroll, *Autobiography and Reminiscences*, 24; McDonough, *War in Kentucky*, 277; Hafendorfer, *Perryville*, 268; *Valparaiso Republic*, November 13, 1862.

203. Maney's report; Malone, *Memoir of Thomas H. Malone*, 132; *OR*, vol. 16, pt. 1, 1,114. At this point in the combat, between thirty and forty Confederates from other regiments had mixed in with Feild's unit. Elias Hoover of the 1st Wisconsin recalled that "the fight was hand-to-hand over those cannon." Hoover, "Battle of Perryville," 3.

204. Otto, "War Memories," 93.

205. "Under This Fire of Artillery," from H.W. Graber, *The Life Record of H.W. Graber: A Terry Texas Ranger, 1861–1865* (N.p., 1916), 174; the statements of both cavalrymen are also quoted in Hafendorfer, *They Died by Twos and Tens*, 722–23; the death of Evans is noted in *Confederate Veteran* 15, "Terry's Texas Rangers" (November 1907): 498.

206. Stewart's report; Hafendorfer, *Perryville*, 259; Noe, *Perryville*, 245.

207. *Confederate Veteran* 16, "Tributes to Gen. A.P. Stewart" (November 1908): 594; Colonel D.C. Kelly, "Lieut. Gen. Alex P. Stewart," *Confederate Veteran* 12 (August 1904): 392; *Confederate Veteran* 17, "Gen. A.P. Stewart" (October 1909): 485.

208. Hafendorfer, *Perryville*, 260; McDonough, *War in Kentucky*, 258; Noe, *Perryville*, 246–47. The 79th Pennsylvania was organized in Lancaster,

Pennsylvania, in September 1861. Dyer, *Compendium of the War*, 3:1,600; Bates, *History of Pennsylvania Volunteers*, 2:1,075.

209. Rebel C. Forrester, *Glory and Tears: Obion County, Tennessee, 1860–1870* (Union City, TN: H.A. Lanzer Company, 1970), 123.

210. Hagnewood and Union soldier quoted in McDonough, *War in Kentucky*, 277; William G. Davis and Janet B. Davis, eds., "The Diaries of William T. Clark," Lancaster County, Pennsylvania Historical Society, transcript in the 79th Pennsylvania Infantry File, Perryville Battlefield State Historic Site, Perryville, Kentucky; Woodward wound information from Holman, Casualties. A soldier in the 154th Tennessee was also wounded by a ramrod at Perryville.

211. *OR*, vol. 16, pt. 1, 1,156; Hafendorfer, *Perryville*, 305–6.

Chapter 10

212. Maney's report.

213. *OR*, vol. 16, pt. 1, 1,157; Hafendorfer, *Perryville*, 269. Maney recorded that throughout the day Turner's battery "bore a highly useful part" in the battle. The brigade commander insisted that the Union troops' "advantage in position and numbers" was negated by Turner's "timely assistance." Maney noted that the attack might have failed had the battery not been present. Maney's report.

214. *Confederate Veteran* 40, "Captain W.W. Carnes—In Memoriam" (July 1932): 245; *Confederate Veteran* 31, "Captain W.W. Carnes—A Worker" (June 1923): 205.

215. *Supplement to the Official Records of the Union and Confederate Armies*, vol. 3, pt. 1, serial no. 3 (Wilmington, NC: Broadfoot Publishing Company, 1994), 284 (hereafter cited as *SOR*); *Confederate Veteran* 24, "J.S. McMath" (December 1916): 560.

216. Hafendorfer, *Perryville*, 306, 312.

217. Malone, *Memoir of Thomas H. Malone*, 133.

218. Maney's report.

219. Tapp, "Battle of Perryville," 276. Terrill, Taylor wrote, sent Garrard's detachment to support Bush's battery because Terrill "was indignant at the conduct of the guns of our Battery posted on an eminence to the left of us about 100 yards, and ordered Col. Garrard to support it." Terrill, trained as an artilleryman, was still focused on the Union cannons.

220. "Medal of Honor Winners at Perryville, Kentucky, October 8, 1862," 1st Wisconsin Infantry File, Perryville Battlefield State Historic Site, Perryville, Kentucky.

221. Hafendorfer, *Perryville*, 271. A member of the 105th Ohio believed that Terrill's enthusiasm for the fight was renewed when reinforcements, like the 80th Indiana, moved to the front. Haver, *Forty-Eight Days*, 37.

222. Faust, *Historical Times Illustrated Encyclopedia*, 748; Philip Van Doren Stern, *Robert E. Lee: The Man and the Soldier* (New York: Bonanza Books, 1963), 92; James Street Jr., ed., *The Struggle for Tennessee: Tupelo to Stones River* (Alexandria, VA: Time-Life Books, 1985), 58; Terrill quoted in *Louisville Journal*, October 11, 1862; Douglas Southall Freeman, *Lee's Lieutenants* (New York: Charles Scribner's Sons, 1945), 1:717n; Constable, *Time-Life History of the Civil War*, 162.

223. Faust, *Historical Times Illustrated Encyclopedia*, 748; Street, *Struggle for Tennessee*, 58; Constable, *Time-Life History of the Civil War*, 162.

224. Lockwood quoted in McDonough, *War in Kentucky*, 279; Starling letter, Western Kentucky University; General Anson Mills, "Union Veterans Talk About Confederates," *Confederate Veteran* 21 (November 1913): 524.

225. *OR*, vol. 16, pt. 1, 1,041, 1,065; Angle, *Three Years in the Army*, 21; Captain Robert Taylor of Garrard's detachment recorded that Terrill was killed while "working the guns" on Starkweather's hill. Tapp, "Battle of Perryville," 278.

226. The day after the Confederate James Terrill was killed in Virginia, he was promoted to brigadier general. Faust, *Historical Times Illustrated Encyclopedia*, 748; *Confederate Veteran* 34, "God Alone Knows Which One Was Right" (June 1926): 234; Mills, "Union Veterans Talk About Confederates," 524; Constable, *Time-Life History of the Civil War*, 162; Street, *Struggle for Tennessee*, 58; *Confederate Veteran* 34, "God Only Knows Which One Was Right," 143.

227. McDonough, *War in Kentucky*, 280; *OR*, vol. 16, pt. 1, 1,156; Mitchell Letter, Perryville Battlefield State Historic Site; Holman, Casualties; *Valparaiso Republic*, November 13, 1862; Starkweather, "Perryville," 2; Pollard quoted in McDonough, *War in Kentucky*, 258. Elias Hoover (Company F) and L.E. Knowles (Company G) of the 1st Wisconsin both commented that since so many horses were killed, the guns had to be dragged back by hand. Hoover, "Battle of Perryville," 3; L.E. Knowles, "Battle of Perryville," *National Tribune* 8 (May 9, 1889): 3. Rousseau reported that Bush alone lost thirty-five horses. *OR*, vol. 16, pt. 1, 1,046.

228. Hafendorfer, *Perryville*, 319; *OR*, vol. 16, pt. 1, 1,156.

229. Stewart's report; Hafendorfer, *Perryville*, 320. Colonel George Porter of the 6th Tennessee reported that they took the hill, "but owing to a strong and destructive cross-fire it was deemed useless to endeavor to hold it." *OR*, vol. 16, pt. 1, 1,115. Colonel William Frierson of the 27th Tennessee also remarked that the troops "were finally drawn off on account of very heavy cross-firing on the left, which, owing to our fewness of numbers, we were unable to prevent." After attacking the hill twice, these men fell back. *OR*, vol. 16, pt. 1, 1,118.

230. *SOR*, vol. 3, pt. 1, serial no. 3, 218.

231. *OR*, vol. 16, pt. 1, 1,065.

232. Watkins, *"Co. Aytch,"* 83.

233. *Confederate Veteran* 19, "Lieut. Charles H. King" (March 1911): 130–31.

234. McDonough, *War in Kentucky*, 278–79; Maney's report.

235. *OR*, vol. 16, pt. 1, 1,114; Maney reported that the regiment's hopes for success "was disappointed [when] the Regt. Bearing the flag was forced back." Maney's report; Toney, *Privations of a Private*, 43.

236. Maney's report.

237. *OR*, vol. 16, pt. 1, 1,156; Seven Walters and Jo Sandin, "Rebel Yells About Battle Flag Held by Wisconsin," *Washington Times*, September 4, 1996; *Confederate Veteran* 13, "Confederate Flag from Wisconsin" (October 1905); Starkweather, "Perryville," 2. As late as 1905, 1st Tennessee veteran Marcus Toney believed that the flag was not captured at Perryville but was instead torn up and taken by members as souvenirs at the regiment's surrender at Greensboro, North Carolina. Today, however, the disputed flag remains the property of the State of Wisconsin. Marcus B. Toney, "Whose Flag?" *Atlanta Constitution*, October 30, 1905. After the war, Elias Hoover and L.E. Knowles of the 1st Wisconsin claimed that their regiment had captured the flag of the 1st Tennessee. Hoover, "Battle of Perryville," 3; Knowles, "Battle of Perryville," 3. Perryville park manager Kurt Holman believes that it was the flag of the 27th Tennessee. E-mail correspondence with Holman, December 27, 2013.

238. Diary quoted in Miles, "Col. Hume R. Feild," 325; *OR*, vol. 16, pt. 1, 1,114.

239. Hafendorfer, *Perryville*, 326; Otto, "War Memories," 96.

240. *OR*, vol. 16, pt. 1, 1,156; Holman, Regiments; Noe, *Perryville*, 374.

241. Noe, *Perryville*, 374; *Louisville Journal*, October 13, 1862.

242. Holman, Regiments; Noe, *Perryville*, 374; Adam S. Johnston, *The Soldier Boy's Diary Book* (Pittsburgh, PA, 1866), 23; Christian Matthews quoted in Williams, "Regimental History of the 79th Pennsylvania Volunteers," 27.

243. Holman, Regiments; Noe, *Perryville*, 374.

244. Holman, Regiments; Noe, *Perryville*, 374; Tapp, "Battle of Perryville," 271. After the battle, Garrard's detachment was broken up. Members of the 7th Kentucky and 3rd Tennessee rejoined their regiments, while Taylor's company joined the 22nd Kentucky Infantry.

245. *SOR*, vol. 3, pt. 1, serial no. 3, 218; Cheatham, "Battle of Perryville," 705.

246. Noe, *Perryville*, 261.

247. *OR*, vol. 16, pt. 1, 1,108; Maney's report; Holman, Regiments; Noe, *Perryville*, 370; "kicked him" from Warner, "George Earl Maney," 133.

248. Holman, Regiments; Noe, *Perryville*, 370; *OR*, vol. 16, pt. 1, 1,117; Cavanaugh, *Historical Sketch of Obion Avalanche*, 219.

249. *Confederate Veteran* 14, "A.J. West, Division Commander for Georgia" (December 1906): 565; Maney's report; Holman, Regiments; Noe, *Perryville*, 370; West, "Great Battle of Perryville"; *OR*, vol. 16, pt. 1, 1,113; *Confederate Veteran* 20, "Appreciated Compliment to a Comrade" (May 1912): 201. One member of the 41st Georgia estimated that the regiment lost four men killed and twelve wounded while they carried the regimental flag. "My War Record," anonymous memoirs of service in the 41st Georgia Infantry File, Perryville Battlefield State Historic Site, Perryville, Kentucky.

250. Pollard, "Brief History of the First Tennessee," 544; Holman, Regiments; Noe, *Perryville*, 370; *Confederate Veteran* 17, "Dr. Lewis Broyles Irwin" (November 1909): 565. It was frequently reported after the war that the 1st Tennessee lost two-thirds of its command at Perryville. *Confederate Veteran* 19, "Capt. 'Dick' Steele" (August 1911): 393.

251. *OR*, vol. 16, pt. 1, 1,108; Noe, *Perryville*, 369.

252. *OR*, vol. 16, pt. 1, 1,108; Stewart's report; Noe, *Perryville*, 370; *Confederate Veteran* 20, "Fatalities in One Company at Perryville, KY" (May 1912): 210; Lieutenant Edwin H. Rennolds, *A History of the Henry County Commands Which Served in the Confederate States Army* (Kennesaw, GA: Continental Book Company, 1961; originally published 1904), 50.

253. Bragg from *OR*, vol. 16, pt. 1, 1,088.

Chapter 11

254. Cameron, *Staff Ride Handbook*, 158; *OR*, vol. 16, pt. 1, 1,056; Noe, *Perryville*, 216–17.

255. For the fight on the Union right flank, see Beatty, *Citizen-Soldier*, 178; Stuart W. Sanders, "Buckeye Warriors at Perryville," *America's Civil War* (January 2001): 38–44, 86; and Kirk C. Jenkins, *The Battle Rages Higher: The Union's Fifteenth Kentucky Infantry* (Lexington: University Press of Kentucky, 2003), 66–81.

256. Cameron, *Staff Ride Handbook*, 177; *OR*, vol. 16, pt. 1, 1,123.

257. *OR*, vol. 16, pt. 1, 1,025; Jenkins, *Battle Rages Higher*, 77; Noe, *Perryville*, 215; Cameron, *Staff Ride Handbook*, 114.

258. *OR*, vol. 16, pt. 1, 1,079, 1,159, 1,111; Stuart W. Sanders, "Every Mother's Son of Them Are Yankees," *Civil War Times Illustrated* (October 1999): 56–57.

259. Casualty statistics from Noe, *Perryville*, 369, 373, and Holman, *Regiments*.

260. Watkins, *"Co. Aytch,"* 81.

261. Noe, *Perryville*, 369–70, 372, 374; William T. Clark Diary, Lancaster Historical Society, Lancaster, Pennsylvania.

262. Maney's report; West, "Great Battle of Perryville."

263. McDonough, *War in Kentucky*, 303; Otto, "War Memories," 100; Noe, *Perryville*, 374.

264. Otto, "War Memories," 99–102.

265. "My War Record," anonymous memoirs of service in the 41st Georgia Infantry File, Perryville Battlefield State Historic Site, Perryville, Kentucky.

266. Walter Jeffers Vaughan, "The Brand of Coward: Masculine and Patriotic Expectations in a Civil War Town" (PhD dissertation, Case Western Reserve University, 1996), 289. Copy on file at the Perryville Battlefield Preservation Association, Perryville, Kentucky.

267. *Confederate Veteran* 17, "Almost Under the Brass Guns..." (April 1909): 163; *Confederate Veteran* 19, "Captain 'Dick' Steele," 393.

268. Carnes, "Artillery at the Battle of Perryville," 9; Cheatham, "Battle of Perryville," 705.

269. Biggs, "Incidents in Battle of Perryville," 142; *Cincinnati Daily Enquirer*, October 17, 1862. For Confederates stripping Northern dead, see also "Dear Amanda" letter, Landrum Letters, Ohio Historical Society, and Robert J. Winn Diary, Ohio Historical Society.

270. Williamson quoted in McDonough, *War in Kentucky*, 290.

271. Mead Holmes Sr., ed., *A Soldier of the Cumberland: Memoir of Mead Holmes, Jr.* (Boston: American Tract Society, 1864), 94–95.

272. Starling letter, Western Kentucky University.

273. *Louisville Journal*, October 14, 1862; Malone, *Memoir of Thomas H. Malone*, 133.

274. Thomas P. Davis, *"Time Wears Wearily On": An Unromantic Picture of the Civil War* (Jacksonville, FL: Historical Records Survey, WPA: circa 1930), 4; Haver, *Forty-Eight Days*, 39.

275. Holmes, *Soldier of the Cumberland*, 96–97. Many civilian and Union accounts describe these pens. See also "History of the 5th Indiana Battery," Daniel H. Chandler Collection, Indiana State Library, Indianapolis, Indiana; Perry, *History of the Thirty-Eighth Regiment*, 39; William T. Clark Diary, Lancaster Historical Society, Lancaster, Pennsylvania. Perryville doctor Jefferson J. Polk recalled the pens, writing, "I saw dead rebels piled up in pens like hogs." Jefferson J. Polk, *Autobiography of J.J. Polk* (Louisville: John P. Morton and Company, 1867), 97.

276. "Most horrid sight" quoted in McWhiney, *Braxton Bragg and Confederate Defeat*, 319; "now held possession" from Chillion Hazzard, ed., "A Broken Link: A Story of the Battle of Perryville," *Monongahela* [PA] *Republican*, vol. 14, January 12, 1865, 2; "in one place lay" from *New Albany Daily Ledger*, October 21, 1862.

277. Fitch, *Echoes of the Civil War*, 62–63.

278. Otto, "War Memories," 96.

279. Surgeon General Joseph K. Barnes, ed., *The Medical and Surgical History of the War of the Rebellion* (Wilmington, NC: Broadfoot Publishing, 1990), 2:254; Loren J. Morse, ed., *Civil War Diaries and Letters of Bliss Morse* (Wagoner, OK, 1985), 31.

Chapter 12

280. Polk, *Autobiography of J.J. Polk*, 98.

281. Holman, Casualties; Johnston, *Soldier Boy's Diary Book*, 23–25.

282. Charles I. Switzer, ed., *Ohio Volunteer: The Childhood and Civil War Memoirs of Captain John Calvin Hartzell, OVI* (Athens: Ohio University Press, 2005), 101; Holman, Casualties. Other Federal wounded from these regiments

were likely placed at the Wilkerson House, once located a few hundred yards behind Starkweather's hill. At this location, in the early morning hours of October 9, Union Brigadier General William R. Terrill, wounded by a shell fragment, died.

283. Cheatham, "Battle of Perryville," 705.

284. Watkins, *"Co. Aytch,"* 83. In his memoir, Watkins mistakenly names Irwin as "Lute B. Irving."

285. *Confederate Veteran* 17, "Dr. Lewis Broyles Irwin," 565.

286. Watkins, *"Co. Aytch,"* 83; *Confederate Veteran* 17, "Dr. Lewis Broyles Irwin," 565.

287. Toney, *Privations of a Private,* 46; *Confederate Veteran* 19, "Capt. 'Dick' Steele," 393. Steele's wound is also listed in Holman, Casualties.

288. *Confederate Veteran* 21, "First Lieut. John H. Woldridge" (October 1913): 503; *Confederate Veteran* 23, "Judge Andrew Jackson Abernathy" (December 1915): 560; *Confederate Veteran* 34, "Mother to the First Tennessee Regiment" (August 1926): 290.

289. Ethel Moore, "Reunion of Tennesseans," *Confederate Veteran* 6 (October 1898): 483; *Confederate Veteran* 21, "First Lieut. John H. Woldridge," 503.

290. *Confederate Veteran* 34, "Mother to the First Tennessee Regiment," 290; W.W. Cunningham, "Mrs. Sullivan, Soldier and Nurse," *Confederate Veteran* 7 (March 1899): 101.

291. Toney, *Privations of a Private,* 46–47; Cunningham, "Mrs. Sullivan," 101.

292. Toney, *Privations of a Private,* 45.

293. Ibid., 44.

294. Ibid., 45; Holman, Casualties.

295. Toney, *Privations of a Private,* 45; Quintard's wartime memory from Noll, *Doctor Quintard,* 60.

296. Toney, *Privations of a Private,* 45.

297. Ibid., 44–46.

298. Fleming, *Band of Brothers,* 35.

299. Ibid., 35, 37; *Confederate Veteran* 32, "Mrs. Florence Goalder Faris" (April 1924): 152.

300. Fleming, *Band of Brothers,* 37.

301. Ibid., 39–40. In the *Official Records,* Major George W. Kelsoe of the 9th Tennessee reported that Hall was mortally wounded. It is an error that has been recorded for posterity. See *OR,* vol. 16, pt. 1, 1,116.

302. Ritchey notice, *Confederate Veteran* 8 (December 1900): 541.

303. Holman, Casualties; *Confederate Veteran* 19, "Judge John M. Taylor" (May 1911): 236; *Confederate Veteran* 20, "Robert T. Bond" (October 1912): 488; *Confederate Veteran* 20, "Robert T. Bond" (December 1912): 576.

304. Holman, Casualties; Fleming, *Band of Brothers*, 35; Toney, *Privations of a Private*, 47; McDonough, *War in Kentucky*, 296; John A. Martin, *Military History of the Eighth Kansas Volunteer Infantry* (Leavenworth, KS: Daily Bulletin Steam Book and Job Printing House, 1869), 21; Wilbur F. Hinman, *The Story of the Sherman Brigade* (Alliance, OH: Daily Review, 1897), 296.

305. Fleming, *Band of Brothers*, 37; pension quoted in David Gambrel, "Last Confederate in Town: Daniel Smith Stayed after Battle of Perryville to Care for Dead and Wounded," *Kentucky Advocate* (October 8, 1995).

306. John Allison, ed., *Notable Men of Tennessee* (Atlanta, GA: Southern Historical Association, 1903), 2:146.

307. Estimates from Larry J. Daniel, *Soldiering in the Army of Tennessee* (Chapel Hill: University of North Carolina Press, 1991), 71.

308. Holman, Casualties.

309. Otto, "War Memories," 102.

310. Switzer, *Ohio Volunteer*, 98.

311. James D. Kennedy, "Important to the Friends of the 105th, O.V.I.," *Western Reserve Chronicle*, November 26, 1862; *Western Reserve Chronicle*, "Battle of Chaplin Hills—From the 105th Regiment," November 12, 1862.

312. Kennedy, "Important to the Friends."

313. New Albany editorial reprinted in *Memphis Daily Appeal*, November 15, 1862.

314. E.H. Lyen, "The Night Following the Battle of Perryville…," *Confederate Veteran* 6 (April 1898): 178; Burnett, *Humorous, Pathetic, and Descriptive Incidents*, 16–17; Edgar L. McCormick and Gary A. DuBro, eds., "If I Live to Get Home: The Civil War Letters of Private Jonathan McElderry," *Serif* 3 (March 1966): 23.

315. Starling letter, Western Kentucky University.

316. Hambleton Tapp, *The Confederate Invasion of Kentucky, 1862, and the Battle of Perryville, October 8, 1862* (N.p.: self-published, 1962), 43n; Daniel, *Soldiering in the Army of Tennessee*, 163; Losson, *Tennessee's Forgotten Warriors*, 73; McDonough, *War in Kentucky*, 295. For information on Bottom and the fight around his house, see Stuart W. Sanders, "Broken in Spirit: Henry P. Bottom and the Battle of Perryville," *Kentucky Humanities*, no. 1 2001): 20–25, and Sanders, "Buckeye Warriors at Perryville," 38–44, 86.

317. *Confederate Veteran* 3, "Graves of Our Dead at Perryville" (December 1895): 1; *Confederate Veteran* 5, "An Article in the *Chronicle*…" (December 1897): 620; Albert Kern, "Perryville Battlefield," *Confederate Veteran* 8 (August 1900): front cover.

Epilogue

318. *St. Louis Republic*, "Died as He Had Wished," February 11, 1901; obituary also quoted in Warner, "George Earl Maney," 134.

319. Warner, "George Earl Maney," 135.

320. In addition to Hardee's recommendation, other notables recommended a promotion for Maney, including Leonidas Polk (April 27, 1863), Tennessee governor Isham Harris (January 27, 1863) and Cheatham (October 11, 1863). George Earl Maney Compiled Service Record, First (Feild's) Tennessee Infantry Regiment, Field and Staff, accessible online via Fold3.com.

321. Warner, "George Earl Maney," 135–36, 139, 144–45.

322. *St. Louis Republic*, "Died as He Had Wished"; [Washington, D.C.] *Times*, "Death Comes Suddenly," February 10, 1901.

323. Compiled service record of George N. Lester, Company B, 41st Georgia Infantry Regiment, accessible online via Fold3.com; *Richmond Dispatch*, "Stories of Confederates," November 23, 1902.

324. *OR*, vol. 16, pt. 1, 1,115.

A NOTE ON SOURCES

B ecause this book uses detailed endnotes, an exhaustive bibliography has not been included. Several sources, however, have been essential. First, the backbone for this project has been the extensive research files located at the Perryville Battlefield State Historic Site. These files include memoirs, diaries, regimental histories, maps, newspaper accounts, letters and more. In addition, computer database files pertaining to casualties and the regiments that fought at Perryville, compiled by Perryville Battlefield site manager Kurt Holman, have also been very useful.

The after-action reports of Maney, Donelson and Stewart were also critical to this study and are found in the Braxton Bragg Papers and the William P. Palmer Collection of Manuscripts at the Western Reserve Historical Society. Other after-action reports and correspondence can be found in volume 16 (parts 1 and 2) of the U.S. War Department's *The War of the Rebellion: A Compilation of the Official Records of the Union and Confederate Armies* (1880–1901).

Several published memoirs and regimental histories were also critical. Confederate accounts include John W. Carroll, *Autobiography and Reminiscences of John W. Carroll* (Henderson, TN, n.d.); John Cavanaugh, *Historical Sketch of Obion Avalanche, Company H, Ninth Tennessee Infantry, Confederate States of America* (Union City, TN, 1922); B.F. Cheatham, "The Battle of Perryville," *Southern Bivouac* 4 (April 1886); Thomas H. Malone, *Memoir of Thomas H. Malone* (Nashville, TN, 1928); Arthur Howard Noll, ed., *Doctor Quintard: Chaplain CSA and Second Bishop of Tennessee* (Sewanee, TN, 1905); Marcus B. Toney, *The Privations of a Private* (Nashville, 1905); and Sam R. Watkins, *"Co. Aytch"*:

Maury Grays First Tennessee Regiment (Wilmington, NC, 1990 [1881–82]). Union accounts include Michael H. Fitch, *Echoes of the Civil War as I Hear Them* (New York, 1905); John Henry Otto, *War Memories* (n.p., n.d.); Samuel M. Starling, "Dearest Daughters" letter, November 16, 1862 (Lewis-Starling Manuscript Collection, Western Kentucky University); Hambleton Tapp, ed., "The Battle of Perryville, October 8, 1862, As Described in the Diary of Captain Robert B. Taylor," *Register of the Kentucky Historical Society* 60 (1962); and Angus L. Waddle, *Three Years with the Armies of the Ohio and the Cumberland* (Chillicothe, OH, 1889).

Three histories of the Battle of Perryville and the 1862 Kentucky Campaign are necessary for anyone trying to understand what transpired in the Bluegrass State in the summer and fall of 1862. These include Kenneth Hafendorfer, *Perryville: Battle for Kentucky* (Louisville, KY: KH Press, 1991); Kenneth W. Noe, *Perryville: This Grand Havoc of Battle* (Lexington: University Press of Kentucky, 2001); and James Lee McDonough, *War in Kentucky: From Shiloh to Perryville* (Knoxville: University of Tennessee Press, 1994). For information about the aftermath of the Battle of Perryville, see Stuart W. Sanders, *Perryville Under Fire: The Aftermath of Kentucky's Largest Civil War Battle* (Charleston, SC: The History Press, 2012). Christopher Losson, *Tennessee's Forgotten Warriors: Frank Cheatham and His Confederate Division* (Knoxville: University of Tennessee Press, 1989), and James R. Fleming, *Band of Brothers: Company C, 9th Tennessee Infantry* (Shippensburg, PA: White Mane Publishing Company, 1996) were also helpful. For an overview of Maney's life, see Seth Warner, "George Earl Maney: Soldier, Railroader, and Diplomat," *Tennessee Historical Quarterly* 65 (Summer 2006): 131–147.

For additional sources, please consult the endnotes.

INDEX

ABOUT THE AUTHOR

S tuart W. Sanders is former executive director of the Perryville Battlefield
Preservation Association. He is author of *Perryville Under Fire: The
Aftermath of Kentucky's Largest Civil War Battle* (The History Press, 2012) and
The Battle of Mill Springs, Kentucky (The History Press, 2013). Sanders has also
contributed to the books *Kentuckians in Gray: Confederate Generals and Field Officers
of the Bluegrass State, Confederate Generals in the Western Theater* (volumes 2 and 3)
and *Confederate Generals of the Trans-Mississippi* (volumes 1 and 2, forthcoming).
Sanders has written for *Civil War Times Illustrated, America's Civil War, Military
History Quarterly, Hallowed Ground, Kentucky Humanities, The Journal of America's
Military Past, Kentucky Ancestors, The Register of the Kentucky Historical Society, Blue
and Gray, Encyclopedia Virginia* and several other publications. He is currently a
public history administrator in the Commonwealth of Kentucky.